Dazzling Quilts

Dazzling Quilts

Easy Glitz and Instant Glamour

Pamela Mostek

Martingale®
& COMPANY

Dazzling Quilts: Easy Glitz and Instant Glamour
© 2006 by Pamela Mostek

That Patchwork Place® is an imprint of
Martingale & Company®.

Martingale & Company
20205 144th Avenue NE
Woodinville, WA 98072-8478 USA
www.martingale-pub.com

Credits

President • Nancy J. Martin

CEO • Daniel J. Martin

COO • Tom Wierzbicki

Publisher • Jane Hamada

Editorial Director • Mary V. Green

Managing Editor • Tina Cook

Technical Editor • Laurie Baker

Copy Editor • Liz McGehee

Design Director • Stan Green

Illustrator • Laurel Strand

Cover and Text Designer • Shelly Garrison

Photographer • Brent Kane

Printed in China

11 10 09 08 07 06   8 7 6 5 4 3 2 1

**Library of Congress
Cataloging-in-Publication Data**

Library of Congress Control Number: 2006008462

ISBN-13: 978-1-56477-669-3
ISBN-10: 1-56477-669-7

Mission Statement

Dedicated to providing quality products
and service to inspire creativity.

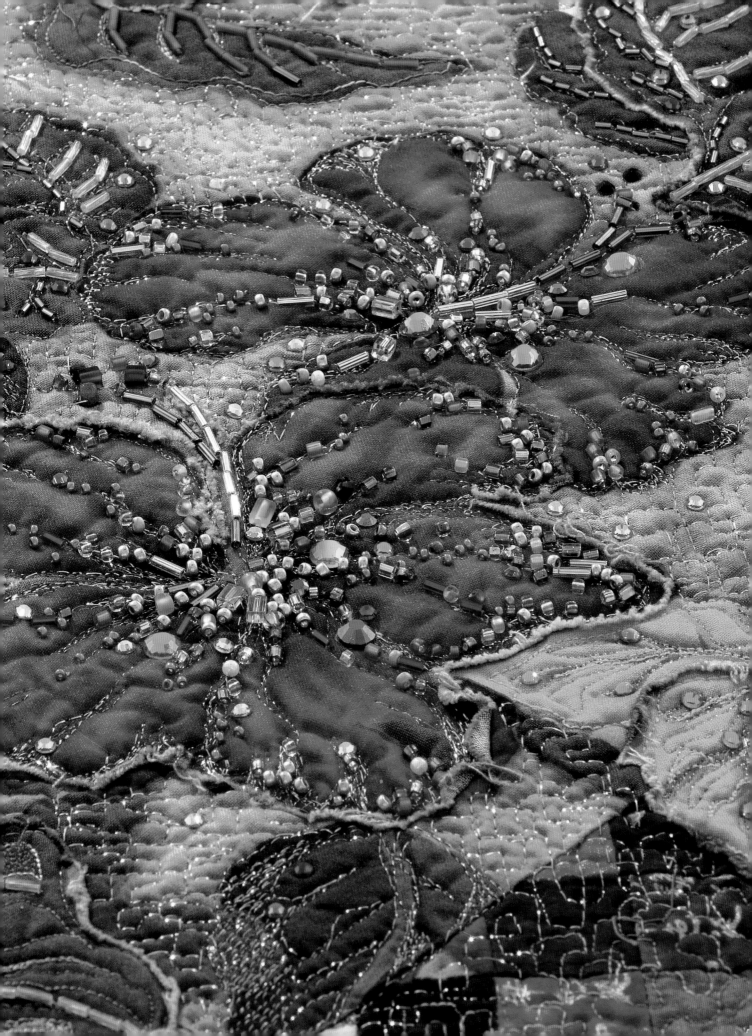

Dedication

To my precious grandchildren:
Jared, Lauren, Josie, and Brooklyn,
whom I love even more than fabulous fabrics, glitz, and sparkle!

Acknowledgments

For as long as I can remember, I've loved anything that sparkles and shines. Combining these dazzling details with my adored, fabulous fabrics has been a delight.

Thank you, thank you to all those who helped and supported me while I worked on this book about quilts with pizzazz:

Special thanks to Martingale & Company, my publisher, who once again had faith in my vision of a successful book. I appreciate their confidence in my belief that glitz and glitter are great things!

To all those who shared their work in the gallery section of the book: Edi Dobbins, Carol MacQuarrie, Debra Lamm, Jean Van Bockel, and Sandy Hawks. All of them did fabulous work, and I'm proud to be able to include it.

To Bernina, for my Aurora 440 with its amazing quilting-stitch regulator. It elevated me from a pretty good quilter with some great ideas to a great quilter with great ideas—all thanks to the machine!

To Sulky, for providing me with a glitteringly wonderful assortment of threads to add sparkle and shine to my quilts. Thanks to Patti Lee, who taught me all the tricks for sewing with Sulky's fabulous Sliver metallic threads. I love them!

To Oklahoma Embroidery Supply & Design (OESD) for also providing me with beautiful threads, plus a fantastic supply of glitzy crystals. Without the crystals, the quilts just wouldn't be the same.

To the quilters who "oohed" and "aahed" when they saw the sparkle and shine of the Dazzling Quilts. I'm very grateful for your approval!

To all the fabric designers out there who've designed and painted the fantastic fabrics that inspired the quilts in this book. Without your talents, there would be no Dazzling Quilts.

Thanks once again to my wonderful family: my daughters, Stacey and Rachel, and my husband, Bob, who just expect that what I do will be great. It's an awesome task living up to that, but it helps me set my standards high!

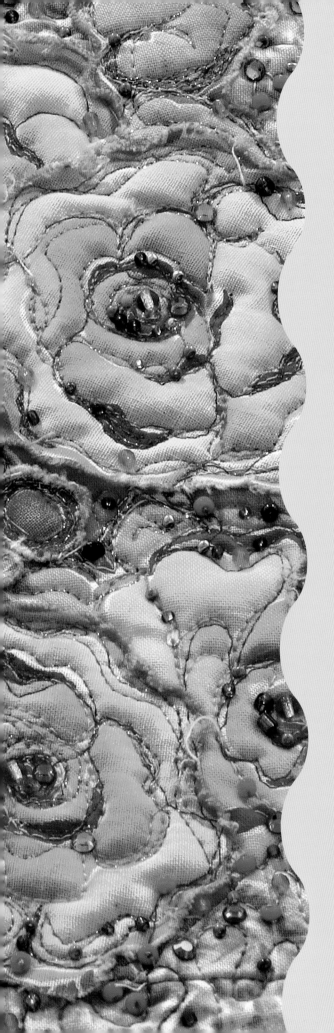

Contents

Further Confessions of a Fabric Lover

I admit it. I'm a total and complete fabric lover. I enjoy many aspects of making a quilt, but I *love* the fabric part—selecting it, playing with it, arranging it, and yes, finally using it to make a quilt.

As a fabric fanatic, I'm always on a quest to use fabrics in a way that shows off their dramatic patterns rather than just slicing and dicing them into little pieces. It was while on this quest that the idea for *Dazzling Quilts* was born.

And it's all about the fabric. Or at least, that's where it all starts as we create a glorious Dazzling Quilt. But there's more. To the fabric we'll add shining threads, beautiful beads, and sparkling crystals. We'll create showstopping appliquéd quilts with sparkle and shine and, most importantly, lots of your own style.

All this glitz and glitter is another of my passions. I love the pizzazz that beads, threads, and any other beautiful bauble adds to whatever they adorn. How fun to add them to a quilt!

In my earlier books, *Just Can't Cut It* and *Scatter Garden Quilts*, I shared ways to use fabulously beautiful prints, especially floral prints. In *Just Can't Cut It*, I designed quilts that focused on amazing fabric in all its uncut beauty rather than slicing those fabrics into little pieces. Then, in *Scatter Garden Quilts*, I

cut those fabrics into pieces, but very special pieces. I fussy-cut fantastic flowers and pieced them into a quilt or used *broderie perse* appliqué to scatter them across a quilt.

I loved the results of both approaches, and I'm excited to present you with yet another way to create quilts that focus on fabric: raw-edged appliqués cut from fabulous fabrics, with a little glitz and glitter for a finishing touch.

If you've toyed with the idea of making an embellished quilt but decided there was just too much to learn to get started, then this is the book for you. You'll find here all you need to know to add a little sparkle and shine to a beautiful, one-of-a-kind quilt.

Or maybe you've even thought of making a quilt that is so uniquely your own it could be called an art quilt. If you have, this is the perfect technique for getting you started on a journey to making quilts with your own distinctive personality. It all begins with finding a fabric that inspires you and letting it direct just how you'll shape it into a magnificent quilt.

Now that you know a little bit about Dazzling Quilts, I hope you'll be inspired to dive right in and get started on one of your own. The process is easy, and the results are so worth it! Enjoy your journey.

Pam

Welcome to Dazzling Quilts

Today's quilt shops, full of dramatic fabrics, are the perfect place to start your Dazzling Quilts. When it comes to irresistible fabrics, large-scale floral prints are my particular passion. But there are other prints that I love as well. Funky fish, exotic elephants, even flying hamburgers—all can be the basis for a one-of-a-kind quilt.

The hunt for that perfect print is one of my favorite parts of the process. In fact, when I see an amazing fabric that I know will be spectacular in an elegantly embellished quilt, I buy it on the spot. Remember, fabric usually isn't on the shelf for long. There's nothing worse than going back the next day for that special fabric and finding it's gone. So, when you see it, buy it! Just having it in your stash gives you time to think about how you're going to use it as the inspiration for your quilt.

In this book, you'll find instructions for eight different projects. Depending on the mood and style of your fabric, your quilt might look entirely different from the one you see in the photo. These project instructions are just the beginning. Study the process section to learn about adding raw-edged appliqué, using decorative threads for quilting and free-motion embroidery, and embellishing with beads and crystals to create designs.

Dazzling Quilts are created in layers. First comes the simple pieced background, then the raw-edged *broderie perse* appliqué in which you'll cut shapes from your fantastic focal fabric. After your background and appliqué shapes are in place comes the fun part—putting on the glitz! You'll learn how to stitch down your appliqué shapes with decorative threads, quilt the background, and then add free-motion embroidery to your appliqué shapes using the gorgeous colors and textures of decorative threads. Finally, you add the beads and sparkling crystals.

Of course, if you prefer, you can leave off the final embellishments. Those finishing touches are all up to you. In "Flower Power" (page 67), I used lots of large, bold beads but didn't add crystals. I felt the playful, retro look of this quilt was just right without the crystals. In "Floral Fantasy" (page 73), I added sparkling rose and green crystals but didn't use beads—just to create a different look.

You'll find some great ideas in the gallery on page 85. I made some of these Dazzling Quilts and others were created by talented friends and quilt designers, who had fun playing with the techniques in this book. I'm so pleased they agreed to share their fantastic quilts with you.

With all this elegant embellishment and stitching, these quilts are designed to be viewed up close so the details can be appreciated. They work best as small wall quilts that can easily find a place to shine and sparkle in your home. Let's face it, even if you wanted to add beads and crystals to a bed-size quilt, it wouldn't be seen and admired by others if it were on your bed. In the case of embellished quilts, small and displayable is definitely better!

I hope you'll enjoy browsing through this book for quiltmaking possibilities. Before you begin, read "The Dazzling Quilts Process," which begins on page 14, then refer to it as needed as you work through the projects. Above all, have fun creating a stitched and embellished one-of-a-kind quilt.

The Dazzling Quilts Process

Dazzling Quilts are individual; they don't come with exact recipes. Each of yours will vary depending on the fabrics you use, the appliqués you place, and the embellishments you add. While there's no specific formula, there is a process I follow each time I make a Dazzling Quilt. That process is outlined in this section.

The Fabric-First Approach

Most of the time when we make a quilt, we're inspired by a photo seen in a book or magazine or an irresistible pattern from our favorite quilt shop. We start with the design and then find fabrics we think will look great with it. Right?

Well, when you make a Dazzling Quilt, you start with the fabric, not the design. Select a fabulous fabric and then let that fabric help you decide how to create your quilt. This fabric-first approach will result in a quilt that is uniquely yours.

Focal Fabric

The first fabric you need to select is the focal fabric. This fabric should be some sort of print, with motifs that can be cut out. I'm crazy about large-scale, dramatic prints with swirling colors and designs, but your fabric doesn't have to be big and bold. It could be delicate and demure if you like. The most important thing is that you *love* the print.

While you're searching for your focal fabric, you want to make sure the motifs in the print don't all overlap. You'll need to cut out motifs to use as appliqués, so at least some of the shapes need to be whole.

Select prints that have some complete motifs.

Avoid prints in which all the motifs overlap.

Once you've found a great fabric, the next question is how much to buy. This depends on the size of the print and the design you plan to use—but you may not have a design in mind when you spot the fabric. Generally, Dazzling Quilts work best as wall quilts so that all the wonderful stitching and embellishing can be easily seen up close and enjoyed. This means they'll be on the small side and use less of the fabulous focal print than a bed-sized quilt would.

If the print is large-scale, I'll probably buy two yards. Remember, you'll be cutting out appliqué shapes from the print, which takes more fabric than simply cutting straight across the grain. The worst thing that can happen is to fall in love with a fabric and, once inspiration strikes as to how you're going to use it, discover you didn't buy enough. To make sure, I always buy a little more than I think I'll need.

If the print of my focal fabric is small-scale, I'll probably buy one yard, but I don't buy less than that. What's left after the project can go into my stash, and I can use it in another project.

Background Fabrics

Even though a focal print is the star of the show in a Dazzling Quilt, I have lots of fun gathering background fabrics too. The background is a great place to work in those specialty fabrics you may have picked up but haven't been sure how to use.

I love throwing in little pieces of hand-dyed douppioni silk, metallics, hand-printed fabrics, and blends of all kinds. There was a time when I definitely would have considered myself a cotton snob, but not anymore. A fabric doesn't have to be 100% cotton to have a place in my quilts. I just have to like it, and the glitzier it is, the better.

While fibers of all kinds are acceptable for the background, be a little careful when selecting colors and patterns. Remember, you want the appliqué shapes to be the center of attention, so the background fabrics shouldn't compete with them. I use primarily solid colors, understated textures, and subtle prints in my backgrounds—no large-scale prints or colors that are stronger than the focal fabric, just fabrics that complement the print rather than compete with it.

It depends somewhat on the design of the project, but generally I use as many different fabrics as I can in the background to create interest, keeping in mind that I don't want to overpower the focal print. In other words, if I decide pink is a great color for the background, I'll undoubtedly use small pieces of 30 or 40 different pinks in different shades rather than three or four larger pieces. In this case, more is definitely better!

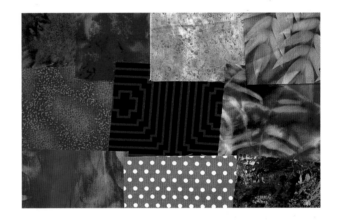

Consider fabrics that are blends or have metallic accents.

The background fabrics shown here would make subtle accompaniments to a floral focal print.

The First Layer: The Pieced Background

After gathering fabric, you're ready to begin putting together your Dazzling Quilt. We're going to do that in a simple system of layers.

In each project in this book, you'll find instructions for a simple pieced background. That's the first layer of your quilt. We'll build on this background, adding appliqué shapes, decorative stitching, and sparkling embellishments.

In many of the projects, the pieced background is a single block repeated in dozens of fabrics that blend with and complement the colors in the appliqué. I've kept the piecing simple so that it doesn't compete with the appliqué shapes for attention but instead creates movement and texture.

A repeated block forms the "Flower Power" background (see page 68 for the full quilt).

In "Sunspot," I used a wonderful leaf print for the border and then stitched raw-edged appliqués cut from the same fabric onto the pieced background (see page 42 for the full quilt).

The Second Layer: Appliqués

After you've completed the pieced background, you're ready to add the next layer: raw-edged appliqués, which will be the focus of the quilt design. What makes these appliqué shapes different from those in other quilts is that the shape is dictated by your focal fabric. You'll use the gorgeous artwork on the fabric, cutting out the motifs and then positioning them just how you want them on your quilt.

Cutting out the appliqués couldn't be easier. Using small, sharp scissors, cut about ⅛" beyond the motif's edge, leaving a little of the background for extra color and texture.

Many of today's gorgeous prints feature more than one shape that you may want to appliqué onto your quilt. For instance, if you select a print with large, dramatic flowers, you may also want to add leaves or other smaller flowers as well. Just remember to select shapes that don't overlap each other drastically. Don't worry if a slight portion is overlapped. Just continue cutting around the shape as if the overlap weren't there.

If you're using strips or pieces of focal fabric in the background, you may want to position appliqué shapes right on top of spots in the original fabric to increase the density or variety of flowers or other motifs in the fabric itself. In a sense, we're redesigning the focal fabric until we get it just how we want it for our projects.

Add appliqués to the focal fabric to create the look you want.

After you've cut out your appliqués, position them on the quilt, using the photo that accompanies each project as a guide. Remember, however, depending on the fabric you've chosen, your quilt may look entirely different from the one in the photo. But this is the fun part! Use the photo as a starting point, not as a complete road map for placement.

Overlap or rotate the motifs until you've created just the look you want. I find that the best way to do this is to pin the quilt to a design wall so that I can stand back and get a better perspective. I then pin the appliqués temporarily in place, being careful to pin them just to the quilt background and not to the design wall too.

To make sure they don't shift, hand baste appliqués in place.

Adding appliqué pieces to the quilt top

Next, I remove my quilt from the design wall, being careful not to disturb the placement of the appliqués. So that the motifs don't shift as I stitch, I then hand baste them in place, using a dark or contrasting thread and a very long running stitch. I make sure that I've crisscrossed each shape with basting lines. These basting stitches can be large and will be removed later.

HAND BASTE? OH, NO!

Oh, yes! Trust me, you can baste quickly by hand. Don't be intimidated by the "hand" in front of "baste." I've tried several other methods of basting and found this one to be the quickest and easiest. Most importantly, hand basting is effective at holding the appliqué shapes in place. As you move your shapes into a pleasing arrangement, you'll undoubtedly end up with a number of overlapping shapes. This makes it difficult to use glue or fusing spray, because you have to lift up sections of the shape to secure it, possibly shifting the appliqués in the process. Small pins will also work, but I don't like taking them out as I stitch. With hand basting, you can just do a long running stitch over several shapes—very efficient and very easy!

Now that you've positioned appliqué shapes on the background and basted them in place, you're ready to layer the quilt top, batting, and backing. Refer to "Making the Quilt Sandwich" on page 91 for tips on how to do this. There are important details to keep in mind, so be sure you read about quilt sandwiches before you assemble yours.

The Third Layer: Decorative Stitching

Once your quilt sandwich is assembled, you're ready to begin my favorite part of the process—putting on the glitz. The glitz begins with threads. You'll first use them for the background quilting, and then you'll add free-motion embroidery to the appliqué shapes.

Before we discuss technique, though, we need to talk about decorative threads. I like to think of delicious-looking threads as frosting on a cake. Even if you don't add beads and crystals—which happens after the decorative stitching—threads can create a perfect finish for your quilt, taking it from "nice" to "very, very nice"!

Just as with fabric, there are seemingly zillions of gorgeous threads available in a variety of colors, weights, and fibers. I've found that many quilt stores don't carry an extensive inventory of decorative threads, and I buy many of mine at online shops. Just one warning: buying threads can be addictive. As with peanuts, it's hard to stop at one!

In this section, I'll describe my favorite threads and give tips for making them work for you. It's basic information, kind of like Threads 101, and it will help you take off on your stitching adventure. If you decide you want to experiment even more, there are many books on threads. I've listed several online thread suppliers on page 95.

CHOOSING THE CORRECT NEEDLE

It's important to pair the correct needle with the thread you're using, or you'll be constantly frustrated by your sewing machine jamming, threads breaking, and stitches skipping. Basically, decorative threads require a needle with a larger hole than you'd use for general sewing, so the thread can easily pass through the hole without breaking or fraying.

Needles are sized according to the diameter of the shaft. The smaller the number, the finer the needle. This is just the opposite of thread sizing, in which the higher the number, the finer the thread. For piecing, I use a standard 50-weight cotton thread and an 80/12 needle. This combination allows the thread to travel smoothly down the front and through the eye of the needle. If a larger needle is used with this 50-weight thread, which is lighter than decorative threads, the thread doesn't travel smoothly down the groove in the needle. The result can be skipped stitches and damaged thread.

When sewing with decorative threads, I use a 90/14 needle. With this larger needle, heavier threads can easily slide down the needle and through the eye. Again, if I used a smaller needle, the decorative threads would rub on the edges of the groove in the needle, possibly jamming and breaking the thread.

Variegated Cotton Threads

These are multicolored cotton threads that change colors every couple of inches to create delightful variations in the color of the quilting. Some variegated cotton threads subtly change color within a given color range, such as shades of greens, while others change boldly from color to color, such as from blue to purple to red. I like to combine a variety of variegated threads in different weights for a little texture.

With variegated cotton threads, you can introduce understated color shifts.

My favorite variegated threads are Blendables by Sulky and King Tut by Superior. There are other beautiful variegated threads on the market, and once you start decorative stitching, you'll have as much fun adding to your thread collection as to your fabric stash!

VARIEGATED COTTON THREADS: HOW I USE THEM

Because variegated cotton threads have lovely color but little sheen, I use them primarily to quilt the pieced backgrounds of my Dazzling Quilts. These subtle threads form the basis for a buildup to glitz and glitter, which is complete when I quilt shinier threads on the appliqué shapes.

I look for a variegated thread that combines the colors in my background fabrics and will work as a blender as it crosses over them. I want to create an illusion of merging, not contrasting. I save that approach for the focus of the quilt, where I want the threads to pop out and shine!

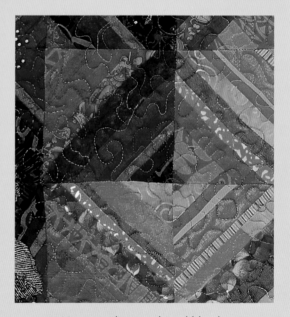

Variegated cotton thread blends with the multicolored background.

Rayon and Polyester Threads

Rayon and polyester threads have more sheen than cotton, and these two types of thread look much the same when stitched. I use them both, depending on the colors I have on hand.

There are slight differences between rayon and polyester, and some quilters prefer one over the other. Rayon has the luster of silk, and some people prefer its sheen to that of polyester. Others see no difference in the sheen. Polyester tends to be stronger than rayon and has more stretch, which means it's less likely to break.

Rayon and polyester threads come in literally hundreds of solid colors. Isacord thread by Oklahoma Embroidery Supply & Design (OESD) comes in every variable shade you might need to create a subtle blend or to contrast with your stitching. Sulky also carries a wide range of both polyester and rayon solid-colored threads.

Because of their sheen, polyester and rayon threads draw more attention than cotton threads.

Variegated rayon and polyester threads are another option. Some, such as Sulky's Ultra Twist, are a combination of two colors. Others are variegated like cotton and come in lovely mixes of colors. Madeira has a wide assortment of variegated rayon thread in both 40 weight (lighter) and 30 weight (heavier). YLI's Pearl Crown Rayon is also a favorite. Signature offers Pixelles, a line of 30-weight, fabulously colored variegated polyester threads with terrific sheen. Superior's Rainbows is another line of gorgeous variegated polyester threads that come in a wide range of brilliant colors.

Step up the drama inherent in rayon and polyester threads by trying a variegated option.

RAYON AND POLYESTER THREADS: HOW I USE THEM

Because polyester and rayon threads have more sheen than cotton, I like to free-motion embroider them onto my appliqué shapes and over focal fabrics. These lustrous threads are nice companions to the metallic threads I also add to appliqués for final glitz.

I sometimes use polyester and rayon threads when background quilting around the appliqué shapes, as a kind of blender between the cotton-quilted background and the sparkling metallics on the appliqués.

Allover quilting in rayon threads unifies the multihued background surrounding these leaves.

Metallic Threads

Finally—the sparkle! When I reach this point in the quilt, I really get excited. I absolutely love adding gorgeous, sparkling metallic threads to a quilt. With these amazing threads, the quilt seems to come to life with a shine of its own.

Just as with the other types of threads we've discussed, there are many, many varieties and manufacturers from which to choose. Even though there are many metallics, they vary a great deal in the amount of sparkle and shine they add to your quilt.

I enjoy combining different types of metallics and different brands to produce varying amounts of glitz throughout a quilt. For subtle sparkle, I like Yenmet metallic threads by OESD. These also come in a twist version with colored threads, which creates a colored stitching pattern with the sparkle of metallic. Superior has a variegated silver and gold metallic thread that is also very nice.

Metallic threads range from subtle glitz to gleaming. Tailor your choices to the effect you'd like to achieve.

When I want the ultimate in sparkle and shine, I use Sulky's Sliver metallic threads, which come in a wide range of colors. This thread is actually a thin, flat, ribbonlike film that's been metalized with an aluminum layer to give it a brilliant reflectivity. Sulky's Holoshimmer threads also create a fantastic shimmer and shine, but they present a slightly different look than the Sliver metallics. Again, I like mixing a variety of metallic threads.

Metallic threads give a quilt extra-special sparkle, but they do require a few adjustments to your sewing machine so that you can sew easily with them. These adjustments will depend somewhat on your machine and the type of metallic thread you're using, so you'll have to do some experimenting until you get it just right. If you have trouble adjusting things so that the sewing goes smoothly, consult your machine dealer or even the thread manufacturer. Both can be excellent resources and save you from working on machine adjustments so you can get right to the stitching!

To sew with Sulky Sliver metallics and other flat, ribbonlike threads, I've developed a few tips that work well for me. First, you'll need a vertical spool holder for the thread. If you're not sure how to add one, contact your machine dealer.

Next, reduce the top thread tension drastically. The top tension should be very loose, and again, this will depend on the machine. With my Bernina, I reduce the top tension to zero (yes, zero!) to use this type of thread, and it works beautifully.

Also, reduce your sewing speed. I set the speed adjustment to one-quarter of the maximum stitching speed, but this will also depend on your machine. Lastly, be sure you're using a 90/14 machine needle. Metallic threads in particular need the larger eye on the needle so that they don't rub against the needle as they go through it.

METALLIC THREADS: HOW I USE THEM

Because of their sparkle and shine, I reserve metallics for free-motion embroidery details on or around appliqué shapes. At times, I simply outline or add lines or patterns to an appliqué, and then I do some more stitching with rayon or polyester threads for the kind of variety that calls out for a second look.

Outlining these leaves and flowers with metallic thread defines the motifs and forms a bridge between the fabric and the eye-catching beads.

At other times, I create solid areas of sparkle by going back and forth over a spot or by laying threads side by side. I save this approach for a superdramatic focus on the quilt. When I use different varieties of metallic threads in different areas of the quilt, I get an interesting pattern of metallic shine that adds movement and pizzazz.

Rows of metallic thread stitched on this leaf create dramatic focus.

Choosing the Bobbin Thread

When you're quilting or embroidering with decorative threads, the bobbin thread needs to be finer—or a lighter weight—than the top thread. This helps eliminate buildup that can occur with heavier bobbin thread. Look for 60- or 80-weight polyester thread, commonly used for decorative stitching. One polyester thread manufactured specifically for use in the bobbin is Superior's Bottom Line, which comes in dozens of gorgeous colors.

I usually match the color of the bobbin thread to the top thread when doing decorative stitching, just in case some of it becomes visible on the top as I stitch. For example, I may be using multiple shades of green for decorative stitching, but a single similar shade of green in the bobbin is fine.

Quilting the Background

Now that you know a little about the threads that can enhance your Dazzling Quilt, it's time to start using them. If you haven't already assembled your quilt sandwich, refer to "Making the Quilt Sandwich" on page 91 to layer the top with batting and backing. Once you've assembled the quilt sandwich, it's time to secure the appliqué shapes. To do this, stitch around each shape about ⅛" from the edge with a rayon, polyester, or metallic thread. I select a thread I'll also be using to embellish the appliqués, but not the glitziest one I plan to use. At this point, you just want to stitch the shapes in place so that they won't pucker or shift as you quilt the background. Because the edges are raw, they'll fray and curl as you work on your quilt, which gives it delightful texture.

Stitch ⅛" from the edge of appliqués.

23

I also make a few stitching lines through the appliqués, such as down the center of leaves or around the individual petals in a flower. This keeps the shape flat and prevents it from becoming puffy as the background around it pulls up slightly in response to heavy quilting.

I use free-motion quilting throughout the quilt, which means I don't draw or stamp a quilting pattern onto the quilt but instead select an overall design and then repeat it. I use simple, overall designs for the background because I want the quilting to add texture and interest but not compete with the stitching in the appliqué shapes. On page 94, I've given you a few designs to choose from. This is just a place to begin, though. Once you start this quilting adventure, you'll begin to see potential quilting designs everywhere—in fabrics, design books, even patterns in flooring! As I mentioned earlier, I generally use variegated cotton threads for the background or perhaps variegated rayon or polyester threads.

Because the projects in the book are relatively small, they're easy to quilt on a home sewing machine. To free-motion quilt, and to do the embellishing we'll talk about in the next section, all you need is the ability to drop the feed dogs on your machine and a darning or free-motion embroidery foot. If you're uncertain about which foot to use, check with your machine dealer or manufacturer for information.

To begin free-motion quilting, hold the fabric with your hands at the sides of the needle and begin stitching. Start in the center of the area you're quilting and work out toward the edges. Quilt all the desired areas around the appliqués, but don't quilt the appliqués just yet. We'll do that next.

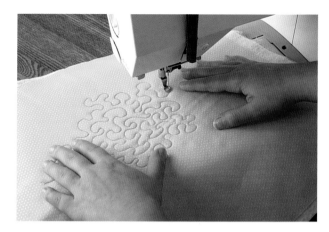

Hold your hands at the sides of the needle.

A LITTLE STITCH IN THE DITCH

Because I like adding lots of quilting and embroidery, I often begin the quilting by stitching along some of the seams. This is known as stitching in the ditch. It prevents the layers from shifting and stretching as I add more and more luscious threads, and it helps me keep the quilt square. I use monofilament thread so that the ditch stitching won't show and interfere with the decorative stitching applied later. This technique is most helpful on larger projects, such as "Floral Fantasy" on page 73 and "Sunspot" on page 41.

Stitch along some of the seams to prevent shifting and stretching.

Embellishing the Appliqués

Once the background quilting is complete, you're ready to start the adventure of embellishing the appliqué shapes with fabulous threads. The exciting thing about this step is that it is soooo easy. The artwork printed on the fabric is the perfect guide for stitching. If you choose, you can follow the color lines and outlines just as they are in the fabric, and the results will be spectacular. It's at this point in the process that I'm very thankful for those fabric designers out there who've made it so easy for me to create an artful, dazzling quilt.

The key to this step is to look carefully at the fabric and decide which sections you want to highlight with more stitching and which areas will have less. I rarely apply the same amount of thread to the entire appliqué shape, because stitching some parts more heavily than others creates movement and a better overall design.

For each of the projects in the book, the instructions include tips on how I embroidered the appliqué shapes. Because your fabrics will undoubtedly be different from mine, you'll have the chance to create your own unique look with stitching. I'm excited for you to see just how simple embellishing is when you use the ready-made stitching guide created by your fabric.

Sometimes the fabric design is so lovely that I embroider only a small amount at the center of the shape, such as a flower, and concentrate the threads elsewhere. Here, I stitched an overall pattern across the pieced background and used minimal outline stitching— and coordinating beads—in the rose.

If I've pieced the focal fabric into the background in addition to cutting appliqués from it, I often stitch the same metallic or rayon threads over the pieced areas that I used on the appliqué shapes. I cut the smaller flower appliqués from the same fabric, applying them over the background print and outlining all the flowers with the same metallic thread.

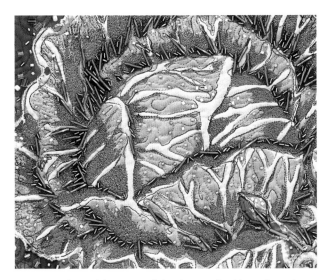

To give this cabbage motif depth, I stitched heavily in the darkest green areas, lightly in the medium green, and left the off-white highlights unquilted except for a defining outline.

The Fourth Layer: Beads and Crystals

Now that all those beautiful threads have been added to your quilt, there's just one thing left to complete your Dazzling Quilt—beads and crystals. As I mentioned before, I like to think of the decorative stitching as the frosting on a cake. Beads and crystals are the scrumptious sprinkles on top! They'll make your quilt deliciously irresistible.

You'll find beads in all sorts of shapes and sizes. Choose colors and bead styles according to your embellishment goals—soft and inconspicuous or striking and bold.

Beads

I love the effect beads add to my quilts. However, I don't think of myself as a beader. I think of myself as a quilter who likes to add beads to her quilts when it helps create the look I'm after.

There are a number of lovely beading stitches and techniques that look wonderful on a quilt, but I use the most basic stitches and approaches when I add beads. I buy beads in the color and size that I like and then sew them to the quilt. Period. There's nothing tricky or complicated about it.

When it comes to choosing colors for your beads, it's good to remember that if you want your beads to really show, you'll need to choose beads that contrast with the area in which you plan to stitch them. If you sew red beads onto a bright red flower, they'll contribute a subtle sparkle. If you were aiming for maximum pizzazz on a red flower, shades of rose, orange, or purple would do the trick.

For most of my beaded quilts, I use two types of beads—seed beads and bugle beads—in sizes and colors that will look best on the quilt. Seed beads are nearly round and are available in several sizes. I just select the bead size according to the size and look of the quilt. Bugle beads are long, narrow tubes, and I use them occasionally as a contrast to the round beads. They're also available in a variety of lengths, and again, I choose them according to the project.

Vary the texture of your embellishments by pairing round seed beads with tube-shaped bugle beads.

For "Baby's Breath Bouquet" (page 47), I used small, delicate beads in pastel colors because the quilt was subtle and demure. Larger beads would have overpowered the appliqué shapes. In this case, I was trying to create a refined, elegant look.

When I shopped for beads for "Flower Power" (page 67), I wanted large, bold beads that would complement the bold, fanciful look of the quilt. Delicate beads would have been lost against the print and colors.

Beading Supplies

Because of the increasing popularity of beaded embellishments on garments and quilts, and of beaded jewelry, beading stores are becoming easier to find. At these stores, you'll find not only a wide variety of beads but also threads, needles, and other supplies that we'll discuss in the next section. You might also investigate the online bead shops listed in "Resources" on page 95. Many large craft stores also carry beads and beading supplies, as do some fabric shops.

In addition to the beads, you'll need to buy several other items before you begin stitching.

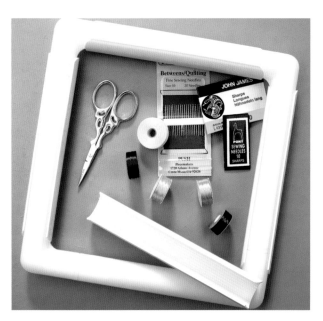

For beading, you'll want a frame, scissors, needles, and thread.

Needles: For adding beads to your quilt, you'll need a thin, short, strong needle. I use a size 10 appliqué/Sharp or a size 10 quilting/Between needle. I don't use beading needles because they bend too easily and are too long for the kind of beading I do on quilts.

Thread: I use Nymo beading thread, which is a strong nylon thread that comes in many colors. There are several sizes, but I prefer size D, which is easy to thread through a size 10 needle. If you have trouble threading needles, you might consider adding a needle threader to your beading supplies. You can buy one at your favorite fabric store.

Generally, match the color of the beading thread to the beads, or use a neutral tan or gray thread. If you find the neutral thread shows a little after the beads have been stitched on, you may want to switch to a matching thread.

Beading Frame: For ease of handling and to prevent puckering, your quilt should be stretched taut when you add the beads. A PVC embroidery frame works well for this task. Position your project in the frame and snap on the side pieces to hold it taut. If you find you need to reposition the quilt for beading, it may not be possible to clamp down each of the four sides because of your prior beading. Securing only three sides works fine, and it's better than fastening the frame over your beading!

PVC frames come in several sizes, allowing you to choose one that best fits your project. Use the largest size that you can comfortably handle so that you don't have to reposition your quilt any more than necessary. Most of the time, I use an 11" x 17" frame, although I have an 8" square that is perfect for traveling. Check your local craft or fabric store for PVC frames.

Scissors: You'll need a pair of sharp scissors to cut your threads. Embroidery scissors work well, and I also use a thread cutter that hangs on a cord around my neck. This way I'm sure I can easily find it!

Small embroidery scissors make it easy
to maneuver in tight spaces.

Adding the Beads

Before you begin to bead, there are just a couple of knots and stitches to learn, and then you'll be ready to stitch.

Begin by cutting a piece of beading thread about 20" long. Thread it through the beading needle and make a knot at one end. Come up through the back of the quilt with the needle and thread, and then tug lightly on the thread to make sure it's secure.

Pick up one bead with your needle and push it down the thread to the fabric. Pull the thread in the direction you want the stitch to go, and place the needle in the fabric close to the bead and perpendicular to the fabric.

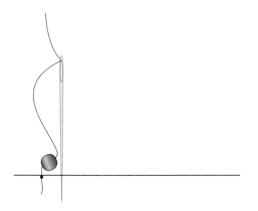

Pull the needle and thread through to the back to complete the stitch. To sew on the next bead, bring the thread up at the place you want to add the next bead and repeat the stitch.

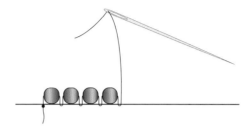

When you have about 5" or 6" of thread left, it's time to tie off the thread and begin another. Take a small stitch very near the point at which your thread came through to the back of the quilt, pulling your thread through, but not all the way through, leaving a loop.

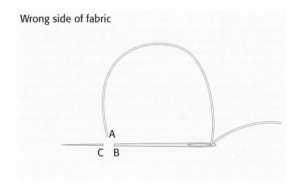

Wrong side of fabric

Go through the loop with the needle and thread and pull the thread tightly against the fabric to secure the knot. Cut the thread, leaving about a ¼" tail.

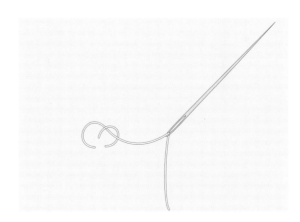

Now that you know the basic stitch and how to start and finish, you're ready to bead. The fun is in creating patterns and groups of beads that form a pleasing accent to your quilt. Place them randomly so that some are closer together than others. Pick up beads of different sizes and colors to create a spontaneous look in your bead embellishments.

I use several different approaches when placing beads. My favorite is to match bead colors to the colors of the appliqué shapes, and then sew these beads primarily to the surrounding background to create a blend between the appliqués and the background. I also do this in reverse, adding beads of the background color to the edges of the appliqué shapes. I think of beads as tiny dots of paint, and I use them to add little bits of color to the background.

If there's a lot of detail and shading in the appliqué motifs, I don't add a lot of beads to them, because the beads would be lost against the busy fabric. Instead, I add a few beads for sparkle and shine, placing most of them on the background behind the appliqués.

In each project, you'll find tips about how I added the beads, but these tips are just starting points. You might find your own approach to beading your quilt. That's the fun of it. Use your imagination, and remember that, when it comes to beads, more is always better than less!

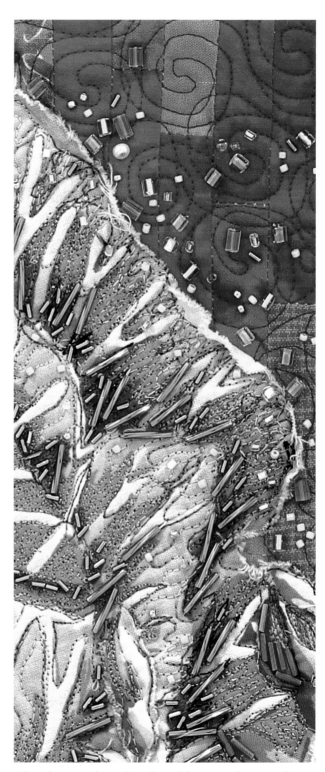

Vary the size of your beads and the space between them.

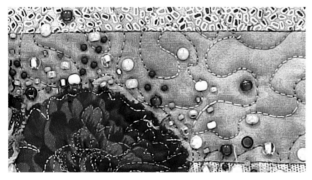

Here I let color variations in the flower speak for themselves and confined my beading to background areas.

I scattered orange and purple beads across the green background to link the floral motifs with the surrounding areas.

If there is bold, unshaded color in an appliqué flower, I might add beads to the flower and not to the background. Here, I used lots of large beads to give the flowers dramatic flair.

Finishing with Crystals

For completing your quilt with the ultimate in glitz and sparkle, nothing outshines crystals! Sprinkling a few crystals across the focal areas of your quilt makes it twinkle with color from across the room. And, the best thing of all, crystals are easy to apply to your quilt. You'll need to buy an applicator wand, such as the EZ Glitzer made by OESD, and hot-fix crystals, which have a heat-activated glue applied to the back. For information on where to buy the heating wand and crystals, refer to "Resources" on page 95, or check at your local craft store.

Follow the manufacturer's instructions to pick up each crystal with the heating wand, let the crystal set for a few seconds on the wand so that the glue can soften, and then apply the crystal directly to the quilt. Once applied, crystals are very secure and can even be machine washed if you affix them to clothing.

To apply heat-set crystals, you'll need an applicator wand.

Crystals are available in a rainbow of colors, allowing you to match or contrast with the quilt fabric.

Hot-fix crystals come in a variety of colors and sizes. I like to add an assortment to my quilts to give different amounts of twinkle to different areas of the quilt. Because of their shine, crystals don't blend with the color on which they're glued; they dominate with their glitz. At times, I add a crystal that is the same color as the background on which it is placed. Their unique sparkle adds amazing drama no matter what color they are.

Crystals are also effective when placed on metallic-thread stitching, because the crystals tend to reflect the shine of the metallic. I particularly like the same color or a similar color of crystal placed on large areas of stitching with metallic thread.

I usually scatter crystals across the appliqué shapes and sometimes the background as well. I use a mix of colors in the quilt that correspond with the threads and beads I'm using. If the colors of the fabrics, threads, and beads are soft and pastel, then I use crystals that are pastel as well.

Matching the crystal color to the quilting thread gives these lines of purple background stitching more weight.

To create a reflected sparkle, dot crystals over areas of heavy metallic stitching.

Now that you know the basics of selecting your fabrics—adding the raw-edged appliqué shapes cut from your fabric, embellishing and quilting with decorative threads, and finally, topping off your quilt with beads and crystals—you're ready to create your own Dazzling Quilt. Choose one of the following projects or create one of your own designs. Just remember to let the fabric be your inspiration.

Little Dazzler

Fabric Selection

For the appliquéd flowers and leaves, I chose a print with flowers that were about 6" across. There were also smaller flowers and leaves in the print, which I used as well. For added glitz, I pieced the triangle border and background from metallic-blend fabrics. I chose a variegated red to complete the border, which gives the quilt lots of color change.

Materials

Yardage is based on 42"-wide fabric.

½ yard of print for appliqués (yardage may vary, depending on the print)

⅜ yard of fabric for center square

⅜ yard of fabric (metallic) for center-block corners

¼ yard of fabric A (metallic) for inner and triangle borders

¼ yard of fabric B for triangle border

¼ yard of fabric for outer border

⅜ yard of fabric for binding

⅔ yard of muslin or lightweight cotton for backing

⅔ yard of fabric for finished back

25" x 25" square of lightweight cotton batting

Variegated cotton thread, rayon thread, and several different metallic threads that coordinate with fabrics

Assorted seed (round) beads in several sizes and colors, including gold

Assorted hot-fix crystals in several sizes and colors, including gold

Finished size: 19" x 19"

Here's a great way to get started. This easy-to-make little quilt will let you zip through the piecing and have fun playing with stitching and embellishing. It's also no trouble to make it larger—just add another border or even two!

Cutting the Pieces

All measurements include ¼"-wide seam allowances.

From the center-square fabric, cut:
- 1 square, 8½" x 8½"

THE CENTER SQUARE

If you are cutting the center square from the same fabric as the appliqué, look carefully at the print to see just what portion of it you would like to highlight for the center. Using an 8½"-square acrylic ruler makes it easy to see and cut around the portion you want to use. Consider which flowers you'll cut for appliqués to add to the center and the border.

From the fabric for center-block corners, cut:
- 2 squares, 7" x 7"; cut each square in half once diagonally to yield a total of 4 triangles

From fabric A, cut:
- 2 strips, 1" x 42"; crosscut into:

  2 strips, 1" x 11½"

  2 strips, 1" x 12½"
- 2 strips, 2" x 42"; crosscut into 36 squares, 2" x 2"

From fabric B, cut:
- 2 strips, 2" x 42"; crosscut into 16 rectangles, 2" x 3½"

From the outer-border fabric, cut:
- 2 strips, 2½" x 42"; crosscut into:

  2 strips, 2½" x 15½"

  2 strips, 2½" x 19½"

From the binding fabric, cut:
- 3 strips, 2½" x 42"

Constructing the Background

1. To make the center block, center and sew two corner-fabric triangles to opposite sides of the center square. The triangles are cut larger than necessary, so you'll have excess fabric on each side of the square. This will be trimmed away later. Press the seams toward the triangles. Sew the remaining two corner-fabric triangles to the opposite sides. Press the seams toward the triangles.

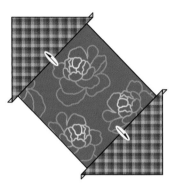

2. Square up the center block to 11½" x 11½".

3. Sew the 1" x 11½" fabric A strips to the sides of the center block. Press the seams toward the fabric A strips. Sew the 1" x 12½" fabric A strips to the top and bottom of the center block. Press the seams toward the fabric A strips.

4. Draw a diagonal line from corner to corner on the wrong side of 32 fabric A squares. With right sides together, position a square on one end of a fabric B rectangle as shown. Stitch on the marked line, trim the square ¼" from the seam line (don't trim the rectangle), and press. Repeat to sew a fabric A square to the other end of the rectangle. Make 16 of these flying-geese units.

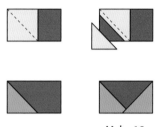

Make 16.

5. Sew four flying-geese units together as shown to make a strip that measures 12½" long. It may be necessary to take in or let out seams if the strip is too long or too short. Press the seams in one direction. Make four pieced strips.

Make 4.

6. Refer to the quilt-assembly diagram to sew a flying-geese strip to the sides of the quilt top. Press the seams toward the center block. Add a fabric A square to the ends of the remaining two flying-geese strips. Sew these strips to the top and bottom of the quilt top. Press the seams toward the center block.

7. Sew the 2½" x 15½" outer-border strips to the sides of the quilt top. Press the seams toward the borders. Sew the 2½" x 19½" outer-border strips to the top and bottom edges of the quilt top. Press the seams toward the borders.

Quilt assembly

Adding the Appliqués

1. Refer to "The Second Layer: Appliqués" on page 17. From the print, cut out the appliqué motifs to add to the quilt center. Remember to cut about ⅛" beyond the outer edge of each shape.

2. Position the appliqués on the center block, overlapping the seam in places with the appliqués. When you're pleased with the arrangement, baste them in place. Press.

3. Refer to "Making the Quilt Sandwich" on page 91 to layer and baste the quilt top, batting, and backing together.

Stitching and Embellishing

1. Refer to "The Third Layer: Decorative Stitching" on page 19. Begin by making the necessary adjustments to the sewing-machine tension, needle, feed dogs, and speed.

2. Use rayon or metallic thread to secure the appliqués through the centers and ⅛" from the edges. This will leave the edges raw to create texture.

3. Quilt the background and add decorative embroidery detail to the appliqué shapes.

4. Refer to "The Fourth Layer: Beads and Crystals" on page 26. Sew beads to the appliqué motifs and background. Add hot-fix crystals for accents.

Finishing the Quilt

Refer to "Finishing Your Quilt" on page 91 to square up the quilt, add a finished back, bind the edges with the binding strips, and add a hanging sleeve.

Putting on the Glitz: Here's How I Did It

I love the softly blended colors in the appliquéd flowers, so I chose to leave the centers of the flowers free of heavy embellishment other than a few scattered beads. I used metallic threads to outline the petals, then added lots of beads and crystals at the tips of the petals and centers.

I used flat metallic thread to heavily quilt behind the flower shapes on the center square. For the side triangles, I added a different type of metallic thread with a little less shine. I quilted the red triangles and outer border with variegated cotton thread in a swirling pattern.

Sunspot

Fabric Selection

For the borders and appliqués, a leaf print is a great choice. You can easily evoke the feeling of swirling leaves as you appliqué the motifs to the quilt. A large-scale floral print would work well, too. For the coordinating fabrics in the blocks, I added small pieces of metallic-blend fabrics, douppioni silk, hand-dyed fabrics, and other specialty fabrics I'd been saving in my stash. Use as many different fabrics and color shades as you can find, but stay away from busy prints.

Materials

Yardage is based on 42"-wide fabric unless otherwise indicated.

1¾ yards of large-scale print for borders, binding, and appliqués (yardage may vary, depending on the print, but extra is included for appliqués)

2¼ yards *total* of assorted coordinating solid or very small-scale prints for blocks

1⅛ yards of muslin or lightweight cotton for backing

1⅛ yards of fabric for finished back

40" x 40" square of lightweight cotton batting

3 yards of 22"-wide lightweight fusible interfacing

Variegated cotton threads, rayon or polyester threads, and several different metallic threads that coordinate with fabrics (your selection should include several types of threads in the same color)

Assorted seed (round) beads in several sizes and colors

Assorted hot-fix crystals in several sizes and colors

Finished size: 34" x 34"

With its abundance of shimmering metallic threads, shiny beads, and glittering crystals, this quilt reminds me of the end of the day, when a little sunlight creates a moment of sparkle. The appliquéd leaves are stitched over the border seam, blending the pieced background with the border. To create a feeling of swirling movement, add the beads in a circular pattern across the appliqués and into the background.

Cutting the Pieces

All measurements include ¼"-wide seam allowances.

From the assorted coordinating fabrics, cut:
- 50 to 70 strips that vary in width from 1" to 2" and are 42" long

From the large-scale print, cut:
- 4 strips, 5½" x 42"; crosscut into:

  2 strips, 5½" x 24½"

  2 strips, 5½" x 34½"
- 4 strips, 2½" x 42"

Constructing the Background

1. Arrange similar colors of the assorted coordinating strips and sew them together along the long edges to make two strip sets that are each 18" x 42". The blocks cut from each strip set will have a different dominant color pattern.

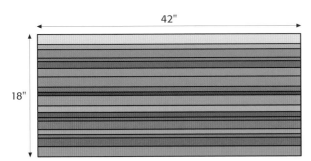

Make 2 strip sets.

2. Follow the manufacturer's instructions to iron the interfacing to the wrong side of each strip set. This will stabilize them so that you can easily cut the blocks on the bias without stretching.

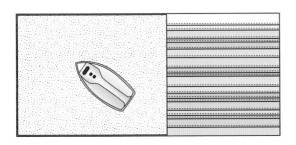

3. Using a see-through ruler and a water-soluble marker, draw a line on the bias grain of one of the strip sets. Measure from the marked line to draw repeated diagonal lines every 4½" for the length of the strip set. Repeat to draw diagonal lines in the opposite direction, making a diagonal grid on the strip set. Cut along the drawn lines.

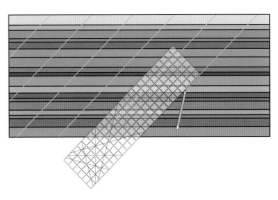

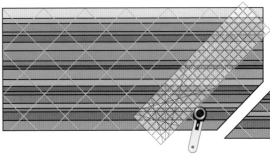

4. Repeat to mark and cut the second strip set. Because you'll have extra blocks, you can choose your favorites and save the others for another project.

Cut at least 36 blocks.

5. Sew the blocks into six horizontal rows of six blocks each as shown, alternating the direction of the blocks so that rows 1, 3, and 5 are the same, and rows 2, 4, and 6 are the same. Press the seams in alternate directions from row to row. Sew the rows together to complete the quilt center. Press the seams in one direction.

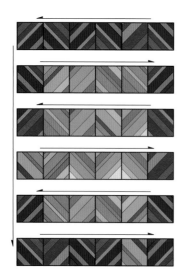

6. Sew the 5½" x 24½" large-scale-print strips to the sides of the quilt top. Press the seams toward the borders. Sew the 5½" x 34½" large-scale-print strips to the top and bottom edges of the quilt top. Press the seams toward the borders.

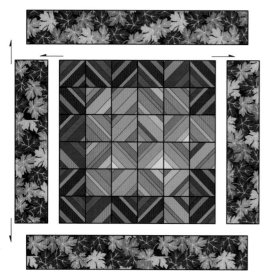

Quilt assembly

Adding the Appliqués

1. Refer to "The Second Layer: Appliqués" on page 17. From the remaining large-scale print, cut out 12 to 15 appliqué motifs. Remember to cut about ⅛" beyond the outer edge of each shape.

2. Position the appliqués over the border seam in a pleasing arrangement that covers much of the seam.

3. Cut out more appliqué motifs and position a few on the background to create a blended look between the quilt center and the border. When you're pleased with the arrangement, baste them in place. Press.

4. Refer to "Making the Quilt Sandwich" on page 91 to layer and baste the quilt top, batting, and backing together.

Stitching and Embellishing

1. Refer to "The Third Layer: Decorative Stitching" on page 19. Begin by making the necessary adjustments to the sewing-machine tension, needle, feed dogs, and speed.

2. Use rayon, polyester, or metallic thread to secure the appliqués through the centers and ⅛" from the edges. This will leave the motif edges raw to create texture.

3. Quilt the background and add decorative embroidery detail to the appliqué shapes.

4. Refer to "The Fourth Layer: Beads and Crystals" on page 26. Sew beads to the appliqué motifs and background. Add hot-fix crystals for accents.

Finishing the Quilt

Refer to "Finishing Your Quilt" on page 91 to square up the quilt, add a finished back, bind the edges with the 2½"-wide large-scale-print strips, and add a hanging sleeve.

Putting on the Glitz: Here's How I Did It

For the appliquéd leaves, I generously piled on the metallic threads, but not to the same level or with the same type of metallic thread for all of them. I selected several areas in the quilt on which to focus and that's where I added the most thread, beads, and crystals. For each of the leaves, I selected contrasting beads so that they would show and sparkle.

Because this is a larger quilt, I added plenty of larger crystals. To create the feeling of movement, I added a trail of beads and crystals that crossed over several leaves and the background in a swirling pattern.

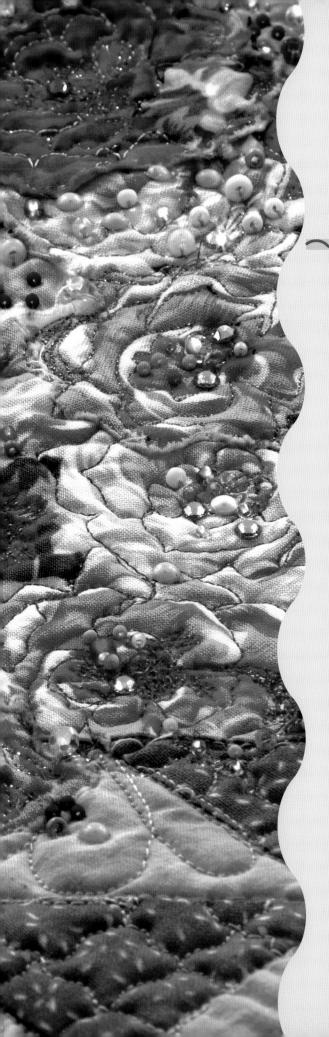

Baby's Breath Bouquet

Fabric Selection

You can create any mood you like just by choosing an appropriate fabric. I chose a subtle, traditional-looking floral print in shades of pink and rose to create a soft, lovely appliquéd bouquet. For the many coordinating fabrics in the background, I chose fabrics that were more softly colored and subtle than the dark rose color in the floral print. Here's a good opportunity to use some of those precious scraps you may be saving. I added little pieces of hand-dyed douppioni silk, metallics, and other elegant fabrics to the scrappy mix of the pieced background.

Materials

Yardage is based on 42"-wide fabric.

1 yard *total* of assorted scraps of light prints and solids for pieced background

½ yard of medium-scale floral print for top of Basket block and appliqués

¼ yard of medium print for basket

⅛ yard of light print for basket

¼ yard of fabric for binding

1 yard of muslin or lightweight cotton for backing

1 yard of fabric for finished back

28" x 29" piece of lightweight cotton batting

Variegated cotton threads, rayon or polyester threads, and metallic threads that coordinate with fabrics

Assorted seed (round) beads in several sizes and colors

Assorted hot-fix crystals in several sizes and colors

Finished size: 23" x 21½"

*Dainty, demure, and elegant—that's the aura of this lovely wall quilt.
The white and pink beads and crystals surrounding the appliquéd rose
bouquet create the look of delicate baby's breath,
adding the finishing touch.*

Cutting the Pieces

All measurements include ¼"-wide seam allowances.

From the light basket fabric, cut:
• 4 squares, 2⅞" x 2⅞"

From the medium basket fabric, cut:
• 4 squares, 2⅞" x 2⅞"
• 1 square, 3¼" x 3¼"; cut the square in half twice diagonally to yield 4 triangles

From the floral print, cut:
• 1 square, 8⅞" x 8⅞"; cut the square in half once diagonally to yield 2 triangles. Discard one triangle or set it aside for another project.

From the assorted light prints and solids, cut a *total* of:
• 6 rectangles, 2½" x 6½" (Basket block and pieced side triangles for quilt center)
• 1 square, 2½" x 2½" (Basket block)
• 2 squares, 4½" x 4½" (pieced side triangles for quilt center)
• 2 rectangles, 2½" x 4½" (pieced side triangles for quilt center)
• 2 rectangles, 2½" x 8½" (pieced side triangles for quilt center)
• 1 strip, 1" x 14½" (first border)
• 1 strip, 1½" x 15" (second border)
• 2 strips, 1½" x 15½" (third and fourth borders)
• 10 rectangles, 2" x 3½" (fifth border)
• 20 squares, 2" x 2" (fifth border)
• 1 strip, 2½" x 20" (sixth border)
• 1 strip, 1" x 12½" (seventh border)
• 1 strip, 1" x 8" (seventh border)
• 8 squares, 1⅞" x 1⅞" (eighth border)
• 1 square, 1½" x 1½" (eighth border)
• 1 strip, 1½" x 11" (eighth border)
• 1 strip, 1½" x 19" (ninth border)
• 1 strip, 3" x 19" (tenth border)
• 2 strips, 2" x 23½" (eleventh and twelfth borders)

From the binding fabric, cut:
• 3 strips, 2½" x 42"

Constructing the Background

1. Draw a diagonal line from corner to corner on the wrong side of the 2⅞" light squares. Place each of the marked squares right sides together with a 2⅞" medium square. Stitch ¼" from both sides of the drawn line on each square. Cut on the drawn line. Press. You'll have eight triangle squares.

Make 8.

2. Arrange six triangle squares from step 1 and the four medium triangles in rows as shown. Sew the pieces in each row together and then sew the rows together to make a large pieced triangle. Press.

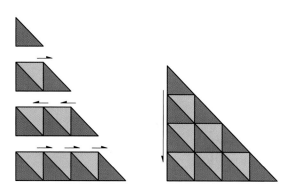

3. Sew the floral-print triangle to the pieced triangle as shown. Press. Square up the unit to 8½" x 8½" if necessary.

4. Sew the remaining two triangle squares to the ends of two 2½" x 6½" light rectangles. Sew one of these strips to the side of the unit from step 3. Sew the 2½" light square to the triangle-square end of the remaining strip. Sew this strip to the bottom of the unit from step 3 to complete the Basket block.

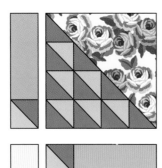

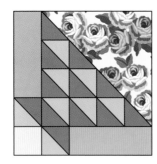

5. Sew together the following assorted light pieces as shown: one 4½" square, one 2½" x 4½" rectangle, two 2½" x 6½" rectangles, and one 2½" x 8½" rectangle. Make two pieced squares.

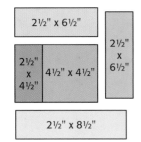

Make 2.

6. Using an acrylic ruler and rotary cutter, cut the pieced squares in half diagonally from corner to corner to make the four pieced side triangles.

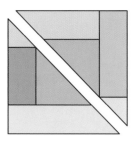

7. To complete the quilt center, sew two pieced side triangles to opposite sides of the Basket block from step 4. Press toward the center. Sew the remaining triangles to the other sides. Press toward the center. Square up the quilt center to 14½" x 14½".

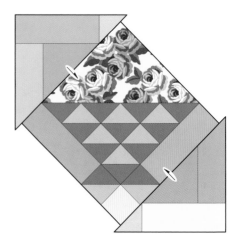

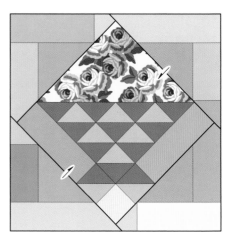

8. Sew the first border to the right-hand side of the quilt center, the second border to the top, and the third and fourth borders to the left-hand side as shown.

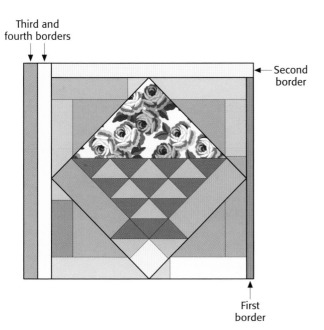

Third and fourth borders

Second border

First border

9. For the fifth border, make 10 flying-geese units. With right sides together, position a 2" square at the end of each 2" x 3½" rectangle. Stitch on the diagonal as shown. Trim to ¼" from the seam and press. Repeat on the opposite end of each rectangle.

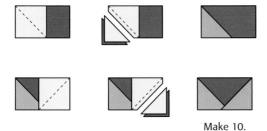

Make 10.

10. Sew the flying-geese units together as shown to make a strip that measures 15½". Sew the border to the right-hand side of the quilt.

PIECING THE FLYING-GEESE BORDER

To create a blended look for the flying-geese border, position light squares on darker rectangles and dark squares on lighter rectangles. Mix them up when you piece them together into a row. If you want the border more dominant, use all light squares on all dark rectangles or vice versa.

11. Sew the 2½" x 20" sixth-border strip to the top edge of the quilt.

12. Sew the 1" x 12½" and 1" x 8" seventh-border strips together to make one long strip. Sew the strip to the bottom edge of the quilt.

13. Draw a diagonal line from corner to corner on the wrong side of four 1⅞" light squares. Place each of the marked squares right sides together with one of the remaining 1⅞" squares. Stitch

¼" from both sides of the drawn line on each square. Cut on the drawn line. Press. You'll have eight triangle squares.

Make 8.

14. Sew the triangle squares, the 1½" square, and the 1½" x 11" strip together as shown to make the eighth border. Sew the strip to the bottom edge of the quilt.

15. Sew on the remaining borders as shown to complete the quilt top.

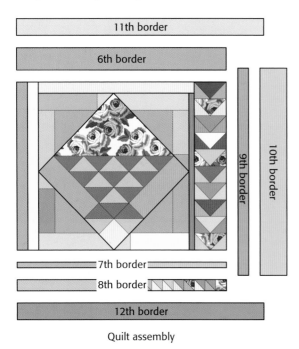

Quilt assembly

Adding the Appliqués

1. Refer to "The Second Layer: Appliqués" on page 17. From the remaining floral print, cut out the appliqué motifs to add to the basket bouquet and to the lower corner of the Basket block. Remember to cut about ⅛" beyond the outer edge of each shape.

2. Position the appliqués on the quilt. When you're pleased with the arrangement, baste them in place. Press.

3. Refer to "Making the Quilt Sandwich" on page 91 to layer and baste the quilt top, batting, and backing together.

Stitching and Embellishing

1. Refer to "The Third Layer: Decorative Stitching" on page 19. Begin by making the necessary adjustments to the sewing-machine tension, needle, feed dogs, and speed.

2. Use rayon, polyester, or metallic thread to secure the appliqués through the centers and ⅛" from the edges. This will leave the motif edges raw to create texture.

3. Quilt the background and add decorative embroidery details to the appliqué shapes.

4. Refer to "The Fourth Layer: Beads and Crystals" on page 26. Sew beads to the appliqué motifs and background. Add hot-fix crystals for accents.

Finishing the Quilt

Refer to "Finishing Your Quilt" on page 91 to square up the quilt, add a finished back, bind the edges with the binding strips, and add a hanging sleeve.

Putting on the Glitz: Here's How I Did It

Because there was a lot of detail in the appli-quéd flowers, I primarily outlined the petals with metallic threads and then added heavier stitching and embellishments at the center. At the lower corner of the Basket block, I stitched the flowers in place with cotton threads so that they would blend into the background, allowing the glitzy flowers in the basket to take center stage.

I used a dark green polyester thread to outline the leaves so that they wouldn't compete with the metallic glitz of the threads on the flowers. I added just a minimum of stitching detail and a few beads that weren't shiny.

White and softly colored beads and crystals were scattered on the background near the edges of the flowers to create a halo effect. Blending the edge of the bouquet with the background contributed to the delicate look of the quilt.

Simply Dazzling Bag

Fabric Selection

When I spotted the fabulous cabbage fabric, I instantly envisioned one of the delicious-looking motifs on the side of a glitzy bag. The flowers are from the same fabric, but you could also add appliqués cut from different fabrics to compose the appliqué arrangement. Just look for a fabric with a large motif that you can use as a focal point. For the pieced background, I used various shades of red with a few pinks thrown in to add pizzazz.

Materials

Yardage is based on 42"-wide fabric.

1¾ yards *total* of assorted fabrics for pieced background

⅜ yard of fabric for bag handles

½ yard of large-scale print for appliqués (yardage may vary, depending on the print)

¾ yard of muslin or lightweight cotton for backing

¾ yard of fabric for lining

2 pieces, 24" x 27", of lightweight cotton batting

Variegated cotton thread, rayon or polyester thread, and metallic threads to coordinate with fabrics

Assorted seed (round) beads and bugle beads in several sizes and colors to coordinate with fabrics

Assorted hot-fix crystals in several sizes and colors

Finished size: 17" x 19"

This stunning bag will be a showstopper wherever you take it. It makes a great platform for stitching and embellishing, and you can change the look entirely by changing the fabric. It's simple to make, and it's easy to adjust to a larger or smaller size.

Cutting the Pieces

All measurements include ¼"-wide seam allowances.

From the assorted background fabrics, cut:
- 60 to 80 strips that are 1" wide and vary in length from 2" to 8". (The number of strips will vary, depending on the length; you may need to cut more later.)

From the backing fabric, cut:
- 2 rectangles, 22" x 23"

From *each* piece of batting, cut:
- 1 strip, 1¼" x 27"
- 1 rectangle, 22" x 23"

From the bag-handle fabric, cut:
- 2 strips, 3½" x 27"

From the lining fabric, cut:
- 2 rectangles, 17½" x 19½"

Constructing the Background

1. Sew the assorted background strips together, end to end, to make pieced strips that are approximately 22" long.

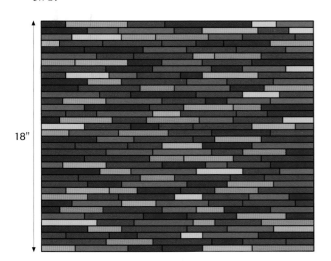

2. Sew the 22" strips together side by side to make a piece that measures 18" wide. Make two.

Adding the Appliqués

1. Refer to "The Second Layer: Appliqués" on page 17. From the large-scale print, cut out the appliqué shapes for your bag. Remember to cut about ⅛" beyond the outer edge of each shape.

2. Position the appliqués on the background pieces, placing them closer to the top and several inches from the bottom and sides. You'll be seaming the pieces together later so some of the pieced area will become the bottom of the bag. When you're pleased with the arrangement, baste the appliqués in place. Press.

CHECK THE PLACEMENT

To make sure you like where you've positioned the appliqués, fold the background in half with the fold at the bottom. This will give you a good idea of how the finished bag will look. It's easy to reposition appliqués now if you aren't pleased with the original placement.

3. Refer to "Making the Quilt Sandwich" on page 91 to layer and baste each bag piece with the 22" x 23" rectangles of batting and backing.

Stitching and Embellishing

1. Refer to "The Third Layer: Decorative Stitching" on page 19. Begin by making the necessary adjustments to the sewing-machine tension, needle, feed dogs, and speed.

2. Use rayon, polyester, or metallic thread to secure the appliqués through the centers and ⅛" from the edges. This will leave the motif edges raw to create texture.

3. Quilt the background and add decorative embroidery detail to the appliqué shapes.

4. Refer to "The Fourth Layer: Beads and Crystals" on page 26. Sew beads to the appliqué motifs and background. Add hot-fix crystals for accents.

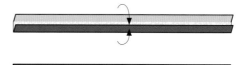

Finishing the Bag

1. After you have completed the quilting and embellishing, trim the two pieces so that they measure 18" x 20". Some shrinkage will undoubtedly take place in the stitching process, so don't be alarmed if your piece doesn't measure the same as it did before. If your finished pieces are smaller than 18" x 20", you'll need to make adjustments to the lining pieces so that they're ½" smaller on all sides than the stitched pieces.

2. With right sides together, sew around the sides and bottom of the bag, using a ½" seam allowance. Press the seam open.

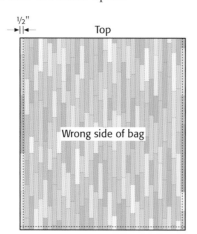

3. With the bag still wrong side out, fold the bag-bottom corners to a point, centering the seam as shown. Stitch across the seam 2¾" from the point. This will square the corners and create a bottom

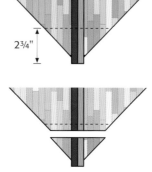

for the bag. Trim off the triangle shape ½" from the seam line. Turn the bag to the right side.

4. Center the 1¼"-wide batting strips on the wrong side of each of the 3½"-wide bag-handle strips.

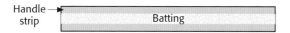

5. Press the sides of the bag-handle strips up so the raw edges overlap and cover the batting. The strips should be 1¼" wide. Stitch close to the raw edge. Press.

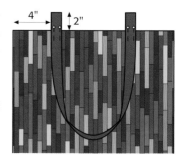

6. With right sides together, sew the sides and bottom of the lining pieces together, leaving about a 6" opening in the seam for turning, and using a ¼" seam allowance. Press the seams open. Repeat step 3 to square the lining corners.

7. With wrong sides together, place the lining inside the bag to make sure that it fits correctly. If necessary, adjust the seams of the lining so that it fits easily inside the bag. Remove the lining and turn it to the wrong side.

8. Position and pin the handles on the outside of the bag so that they're 4" from the side seams, with about 2" at each end extending beyond the top of the bag.

9. With right sides together, place the bag inside the lining. The wrong side of the lining will be facing out. Stitch ½" from the top raw edges.

10. Carefully pull the bag through the opening in the side of the lining so that the outside of the bag is to the outside. Adjust the lining, press the seams carefully, and topstitch ½" from the top of the bag. Slipstitch the lining opening closed.

Putting on the Glitz: Here's How I Did It

The cabbage motif from this fabric made it very easy to decide just where and what to add for embellishments. I used the lines of the cabbage as a guide. In the shaded areas of the leaves, I layered on the metallic thread and then added glitzy green bugle beads to further define the shadows.

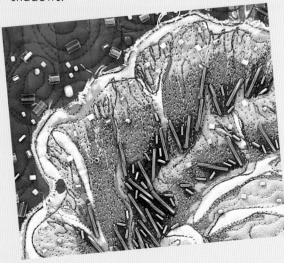

Because the veins of the cabbage are white, I wanted them to pop out just like on a real cabbage. I outlined the veins with variegated rayon thread and then added more metallic thread to the area behind the veins.

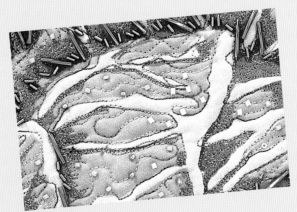

I added light pink and green beads to the outer edges of the leaves and also scattered larger green and pink beads on the background around the cabbage. This technique creates a blended effect between the appliqué shapes and the background.

Because of the many seams in the bag, I quilted it in a small-scale, overall pattern that went back and forth repeatedly over those seams to keep the bag flat and give the bag body. I quilted in a spiral pattern that you can see on page 94. If you want the quilting on your bag to show a little more, try quilting it with a variegated polyester thread, such as Signature's Pixelles.

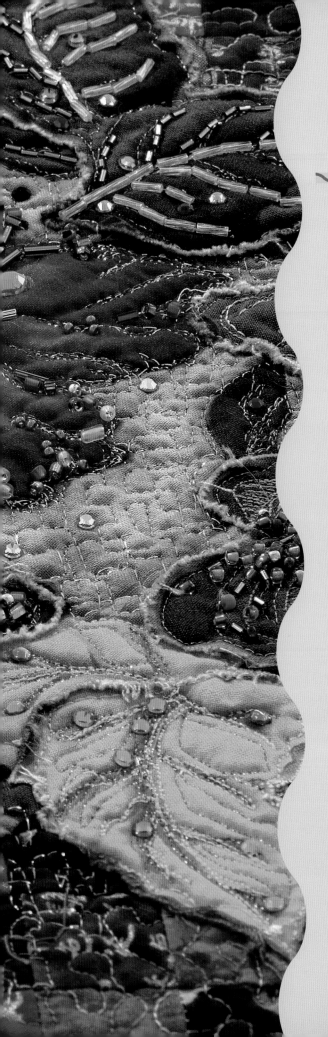

Garden of Gold

Fabric Selection

The appliqués were cut from an exotic, jungle-looking print that I absolutely loved. I didn't use this print for the center square background, however. Instead, I chose a deep gold that looked fabulous with gold metallic threads added to it. The checkerboard squares on the sides of the center square are composed of a variety of metallic and glitzy fabrics that coordinate but don't compete with the appliqués. The narrow borders also include lots of fabric with gold metallic accents, which adds to the overall golden glow of the quilt. To finish, I added an outer border of black strips cut in two different widths.

Materials

Yardage is based on 42"-wide fabric.

Approximately 1 yard *total* of assorted coordinating prints and solids for checkerboard side triangles and narrow borders

½ yard of large-scale print for appliqués (yardage may vary, depending on the print)

½ yard of fabric for center square

⅜ yard of fabric for outer border

¼ yard of fabric for inner border

⅜ yard of fabric for binding

1 yard of muslin or lightweight cotton for backing

1 yard of fabric for finished back

31" x 32" piece of lightweight cotton batting

Variegated cotton thread, rayon or polyester thread, and several different metallic threads, including gold, to coordinate with fabrics

Assorted seed (round) beads and bugle beads in several sizes and colors, including gold

Assorted hot-fix crystals in several sizes and colors, including gold

Finished size: 27" x 25½"

More sparkle and glitz is definitely better in this easy-to-piece and gorgeous-to-look-at wall quilt. It's also easy to change the size and shape by adding more or fewer narrow borders.

Cutting the Pieces

All measurements include ¼"-wide seam allowances.

From the assorted prints and solids, cut:
- 1 strip, 1½" x 42"
- 17 strips, 1" x 42"
- 144 squares, 1½" x 1½"

From the center-square fabric, cut:
- 1 square, 11¾" x 11¾"

From the inner-border fabric, cut:
- 2 strips, 2" x 42"; crosscut into:
  2 strips, 2" x 16½"
  2 strips, 2" x 19½"

From the outer-border fabric, cut:
- 1 strip, 2½" x 42"
- 3 strips, 1½" x 42"

From the binding fabric, cut:
- 4 strips, 2" x 42"

Constructing the Background

1. Arrange the 1½" assorted squares into eight rows as shown, beginning with eight squares in the first row and deleting one square from each of the subsequent rows. Sew the squares in each row together. Press the seams in opposite directions from row to row. Sew the rows together to form a triangle with stair-stepped edges. Press the seams in one direction. Make four.

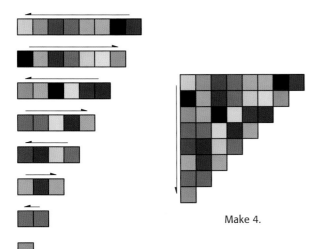

Make 4.

2. Using an acrylic ruler and rotary cutter, trim the stair-stepped edge of each triangle as shown.

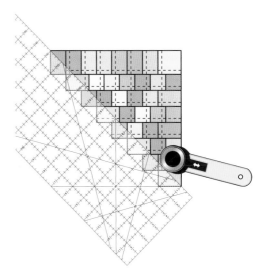

3. Sew two pieced triangles to opposite sides of the 11¾" center square. Press the seams toward the center square. Sew the remaining triangles to the other sides. Press the seams toward the center square. The square should measure 16½" x 16½".

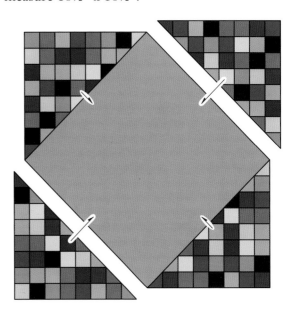

4. Sew the 2" x 16½" inner-border strips to the sides of the quilt center. Press. Sew the 2" x 19½" inner-border strips to the top and bottom edges of the quilt center. Press.

5. Measure the length of the quilt top through the center. From the assorted 1" x 42" strips, cut two strips to the length measured. Sew them to the sides of the quilt top. Measure the width of the quilt top through the center. From the remaining assorted strips, cut two strips to the length measured. Sew these strips to the top and bottom edges of the quilt top. Repeat to add three border strips to each side of the quilt top.

6. Add another border to the left-hand side and then the bottom edge. Repeat two more times until you have a total of six borders on the left-hand side and bottom, using the remaining assorted 1" x 42" and 1½" x 42" strips.

7. Refer to step 5 to measure the length of the quilt top through the center. Trim the 2½" x 42" outer-border strip to this measurement and sew it to the left-hand side of the quilt top. Trim a 1½" x 42" outer-border strip to the same measurement and sew it to the right-hand side of the quilt top. Measure the width of the quilt top through the center and trim the remaining two 1½" x 42" outer-border strips to this measurement. Sew the strips to the top and bottom edges of the quilt top.

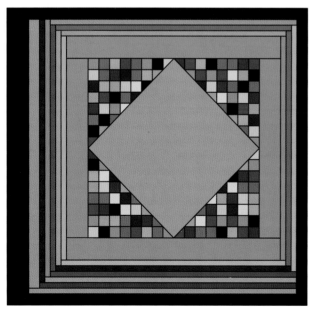

Quilt assembly

Adding the Appliqués

1. Refer to "The Second Layer: Appliqués" on page 17. From the large-scale print fabric, cut out the appliqué motifs that you will add to the quilt center. Remember to cut about ⅛" beyond the outer edge of each shape.

2. Position the appliqués on the center portion of the quilt. Overlap many of them into the pieced background. When you are pleased with the arrangement, baste them in place. Press.

3. Refer to "Making the Quilt Sandwich" on page 91 to layer and baste the quilt top, batting, and backing together.

Stitching and Embellishing

1. Refer to "The Third Layer: Decorative Stitching" on page 19. Begin by making the necessary adjustments to the sewing-machine tension, needle, feed dogs, and speed.

2. Use rayon, polyester, or metallic thread to secure the appliqués through the centers and ⅛" from the edges. This will leave the motif edges raw to create texture.

3. Quilt the background and add decorative embroidery detail to the appliqué shapes.

4. Refer to "The Fourth Layer: Beads and Crystals" on page 26. Sew beads to the appliqué motifs and background. Add hot-fix crystals for accents.

Finishing the Quilt

Refer to "Finishing Your Quilt" on page 91 to square up the quilt and add the finished back. Use the raw-edge technique to bind the edges with the binding strips. Add a hanging sleeve.

Putting on the Glitz: Here's How I Did It

On this project, I really piled on the glitz and glitter! I stitched the background with a very small overall pattern using Sulky Sliver metallic threads for the ultimate in sparkle. I used variegated cotton thread in the border areas and gradually blended the different threads in the pieced corner triangles.

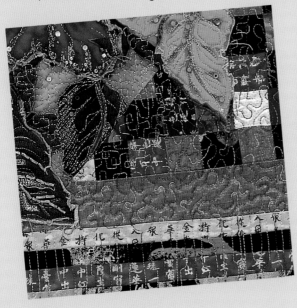

Bugle beads were used to outline the veins in the leaves and the flower details. The results definitely call for a second look!

I used metallic threads to give detail to the flowers and primarily used variegated polyester thread on the leaves. Because the flowers are big and bold, I used mostly large beads and crystals in the center of the flowers with smaller ones at the tips. The beads and crystals are heaviest in the flower centers and edges, leaving much of the flower petals without beads to give the illusion that the center is the lightest part of the leaf—kind of like painting with beads!

Flower Power

Fabric Selection

Because the motifs in my focal fabric were primarily bold shapes of bright pink, orange, and red, I pieced the background from many different shades of bright pink and orange. I used small pieces of specialty fabrics, such as silks and metallics, and a few prints with various shades of orange or pink. Because orange and pink were still too dominant, after I positioned the appliqué shapes, I cut out and added more red flowers on top of the print so they would dominate.

Materials

Yardage is based on 42"-wide fabric.

1½ yards of large-scale floral print for background strips, appliqués, and binding (yardage may vary, depending on the print, but extra has been added for appliqués)

⅔ yard *total* of assorted pink fabrics for background blocks

⅓ yard *total* of assorted orange fabrics for background blocks

⅛ yard *each* of 3 pink fabrics for borders and binding

⅛ yard *each* of 3 orange fabrics for borders and binding

1 yard of muslin or lightweight cotton for backing

1 yard of fabric for finished back

34" x 46" piece of lightweight cotton batting

Variegated cotton threads, rayon or polyester threads, and metallic threads to coordinate with fabrics

Assorted large round beads to coordinate with fabrics

Finished size: 28" x 40"

This bright, playful quilt reminds me of the colors and shapes of the '60s, thus the name. The background is made up of strips of the focal fabric and strips of Hourglass blocks pieced from many pink and orange fabrics, which blend from top to bottom.

Cutting the Pieces

All measurements include ¼"-wide seam allowances.

From the assorted pink fabrics for background blocks, cut a *total* of:
• 64 squares, 3¼" x 3¼"

From the assorted orange fabrics for background blocks, cut a *total* of:
• 34 squares, 3¼" x 3¼"

From the pink fabrics for borders and binding, cut a *total* of:
• 2 strips, 1½" x 28½"
• 1 strip, 2½" x 28½"
• 1 strip, 2" x 42"

From the orange fabrics for borders and binding, cut a *total* of:
• 2 strips, 1½" x 28½"
• 1 strip, 2½" x 28½"
• 1 strip, 2" x 42"

From the floral print, cut:
• 2 strips, 6½" x 32½"
• 2 strips, 2½" x 32½"
• 2 strips, 2" x 42"

Constructing the Background

1. On the wrong side of half of the pink squares, draw a diagonal line from corner to corner. Place each of the marked pink squares right sides together with a different remaining pink square. Stitch ¼" from each side of the diagonal line on each square. Cut on the drawn lines. Press. You'll have 64 triangle squares.

Make 64.

2. On the wrong side of half of the triangle squares, draw a diagonal line that is perpendicular to the existing seam line. Place each of the marked squares right sides together with one of the remaining triangle squares, aligning the seam lines. Pair different fabric combinations when possible. Stitch ¼" from each side of the drawn line. Cut on the drawn line. Press. You'll have 64 quarter-square triangles. You'll use 63. Discard one of the quarter-square triangles or set it aside to use in another project.

Make 64.

3. Repeat steps 1 and 2 with the orange squares to make 34 quarter-square triangles. You'll use 33. Discard one of the quarter-square triangles or set it aside to use in another project.

4. Sew a pink quarter-square triangle to an orange quarter-square triangle. Make three.

Make 3.

5. Sew the remaining pink quarter-square triangles together in pairs. Repeat with the remaining orange quarter-square triangles. You'll have 30 pink units and 15 orange units.

6. Arrange the paired quarter-square-triangle units into three strips of 16 pairs, placing the pink units at the top, the orange units at the bottom, and a pink-and-orange unit between the two colors. Adjust the number of pink and orange units in each strip until you're pleased with the arrangement.

7. Sew the floral-print 32½"-long strips and the quarter-square-triangle strips together in vertical rows as shown. Press the seams toward the floral-print strips.

8. Sew the pink 1½" x 28½" strips together along the long edges. Add the pink 2½" x 28½" strip to the pair to complete the top border. Repeat with the orange 1½" x 28½" and 2½" x 28½" strips to complete the bottom border. Sew the pink and orange border units to the top and bottom edges of the vertical strip unit as shown. Press toward the borders.

Make 3.

Quilt assembly

Adding the Appliqués

1. Refer to "The Second Layer: Appliqués" on page 17. From the remaining floral print, cut out the appliqué motifs that you'll add to the quilt. Remember to cut about ⅛" beyond the outer edge of each shape.

2. Position the appliqués on the floral-print strips, overlapping onto the background and top and bottom borders. When you're pleased with the arrangement, baste them in place. Press.

3. Refer to "Making the Quilt Sandwich" on page 91 to layer and baste the quilt top, batting, and backing together.

Stitching and Embellishing

1. Refer to "The Third Layer: Decorative Stitching" on page 19. Begin by making the necessary adjustments to the sewing-machine tension, needle, feed dogs, and speed.

2. Use rayon, polyester, or metallic thread to secure the appliqués through the centers and ⅛" from the edges. This will leave the motif edges raw to create texture.

3. Quilt the pieced and print background strips, and add decorative embroidery detail to the appliqué shapes.

4. Refer to "The Fourth Layer: Beads and Crystals" on page 26. Sew beads to the appliqué motifs and background. Add hot-fix crystals for accents if desired.

Finishing the Quilt

Refer to "Finishing Your Quilt" on page 91 to square up the quilt and add the finished back. Use the raw-edge binding technique on page 93 to bind the quilt sides with the 2"-wide floral-print strips, the top edge with the 2"-wide pink strip, and the bottom edge with the 2"-wide orange strip. Add a hanging sleeve.

Putting on the Glitz: Here's How I Did It

In the pieced background strips, I used variegated pink and orange cotton threads to heavily quilt in an overall pattern because of the many seams. In the print background areas, I used glitzy Sulky Holoshimmer and Sliver metallic threads to outline the leaves and flowers and quilt the background. I also used the same metallic threads to outline the flower petals although I didn't add embroidery to the flower petals.

With the bright, clear colors of the flowers, the beading showed up very nicely, so I stitched on large white beads for high contrast with the red flowers. I sewed a variety of large beads to the flower centers. Because of the overall funky, retro look of the quilt, I thought it was more effective without crystals. With another print, however, the crystals could be a wonderful finishing touch.

Floral Fantasy

Fabric Selection

Creating this quilt was particularly fun, because all the fabrics are ones I designed, and I thought they created a wonderful fantasy wreath of flowers. The outer border is a smaller companion print to the larger floral print in the center, but the large floral easily dominates and doesn't compete with the border print. If you select a print for the outer border, make sure the large-print focal fabric will still be the center of attention. The center green square and first border are both from the same variegated green, which helps create an illusion of blending as the colors lighten and darken.

Materials

Yardage is based on 42"-wide fabric.

1⅔ yards of large-scale floral print for wreath and appliqués (yardage may vary, depending on the print, but extra is included for appliqués)

⅔ yard of fabric for center square and first border

½ yard of fabric for second and checkerboard borders

⅜ yard of fabric for third and checkerboard borders

⅝ yard of fabric for outer border

⅜ yard of fabric for binding

3 yards of fabric for backing

3 yards of fabric for finished back

47" x 47" piece of lightweight cotton batting

Variegated cotton thread and metallic thread to coordinate with fabrics

Assorted hot-fix crystals in several sizes and colors

Finished size: 41" x 41"

In this easy-to-piece quilt, the sparkle of crystals and metallic threads creates a fantasy look. A dramatic floral print is used for the center border, and appliquéd flowers and leaves cut from the same fabric spill out from the center and appear again at the corners of the borders. Easy to piece—and lovely to look at.

Cutting the Pieces

All measurements include ¼"-wide seam allowances.

From the floral print, cut:
- 2 strips, 6½" x 42"; crosscut into:
  2 rectangles, 6½" x 9½"
  2 strips, 6½" x 21½"

From the fabric for center square and first border, cut:
- 2 strips, 2½" x 21½"
- 2 strips, 2½" x 25½"
- 1 square, 9½" x 9½"

From the fabric for second and checkerboard borders, cut:
- 2 strips, 2½" x 25½"
- 2 strips, 2½" x 29½"
- 3 strips, 1½" x 42"

From the fabric for third and checkerboard borders, cut:
- 3 strips, 1½" x 42"
- 2 strips, 1½" x 31½"
- 2 strips, 1½" x 33½"

From the outer-border fabric, cut:
- 2 strips, 4½" x 33½"
- 2 strips, 4½" x 41½"

From the binding fabric, cut
- 5 strips, 2½" x 42"

Constructing the Background

1. Sew the 6½" x 9½" floral-print rectangles to the sides of the 9½" center square. Press. Sew the 6½" x 21½" floral print strips to the top and bottom. Press.

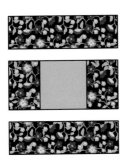

2. Sew the 2½" x 21½" first-border strips to the sides of the center unit and the 2½" x 25½" first-border strips to the top and bottom. Sew the 2½" x 25½" second-border strips to the sides and then add the 2½" x 29½" second-border strips to the top and bottom.

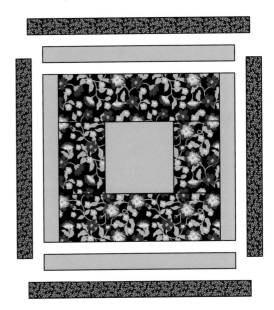

3. To make the checkerboard border, sew the 1½" x 42" checkerboard-border strips together to make a strip set as shown. Press. Cut the strip set into 20 segments, 1½" wide.

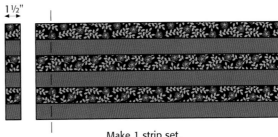

1½"

Make 1 strip set.
Cut 20 segments.

4. Sew five segments from step 3 together, end to end, as shown. Remove one square from the end of the strip and set it aside. Make two strips. Sew the strips to the sides of the quilt.

Remove
1 square.

Side border.
Make 2.

ADJUSTING THE SEAMS

If your checkerboard-border strip is slightly long or short, take in or let out a few of the seams until it measures the same as the border to which you're sewing it. When I'm making a strip set like this, I usually take a slightly scant ¼" seam because I'd much rather take a seam in a little than let it out!

5. Repeat step 4 to sew five segments together, end to end, but don't remove the square. Sew the squares that you removed from the side borders to one end of each of the strips, making sure the colors alternate. Sew these strips to the top and bottom of the quilt.

Add
square.

Top/bottom border.
Make 2.

6. Sew the 1½" x 31½" third-border strips to the sides of the quilt and then add the 1½" x 33½" third-border strips to the top and bottom. Press toward the strips. Sew the 4½" x 33½" outer-border strips to the sides and then sew the 4½" x 41½" outer-border strips to the top and bottom. Press toward the strips.

Quilt assembly

Adding the Appliqués

1. Refer to "The Second Layer: Appliqués" on page 17. From the remaining floral print, cut out the appliqué motifs for the floral wreath. Remember to cut about ⅛" beyond the outer edge of each shape.

2. Position the appliqués on the quilt top over the seams of the floral-print pieces. In addition, you may want to add appliqués on top of the floral pieces if you feel too much of the print background is showing through. Position additional motifs at the corners of the third border, overlapping them onto the other inner borders as well as the outer border. When you're pleased with the arrangement, baste them in place. Press.

3. Refer to "Making the Quilt Sandwich" on page 91 to layer and baste the quilt top, batting, and backing together.

Stitching and Embellishing

1. Refer to "The Third Layer: Decorative Stitching" on page 19. Begin by making the necessary adjustments to the sewing-machine tension, needle, feed dogs, and speed.

2. Use metallic thread to secure the appliqués through the centers and ⅛" from the edges. This will leave the motif edges raw to create texture.

3. Quilt the background and add decorative embroidery detail to the appliqués.

4. Refer to "The Fourth Layer: Beads and Crystals" on page 26. Add hot-fix crystals to the appliquéd wreath flowers and background.

Finishing the Quilt

Refer to "Finishing Your Quilt" on page 91 to square up the quilt, add a finished back, bind the edges with the binding strips, and add a hanging sleeve.

Putting on the Glitz: Here's How I Did It

Because I thought that too much of the black background was visible after I appliquéd flowers around the edge and on the seams, I also added more appliquéd flowers on top of the print itself to give a more concentrated look to the flowers. Then I stitched metallic lines through the black to add a little sparkle and interest.

For a different look, I added lots of hot-fix crystals in the colors of the fabrics but omitted the beads. I also used only metallic threads in the embroidery on the appliqués for a little more glitz. The sparkling crystals looked great sprinkled across the background as well as on the appliqués.

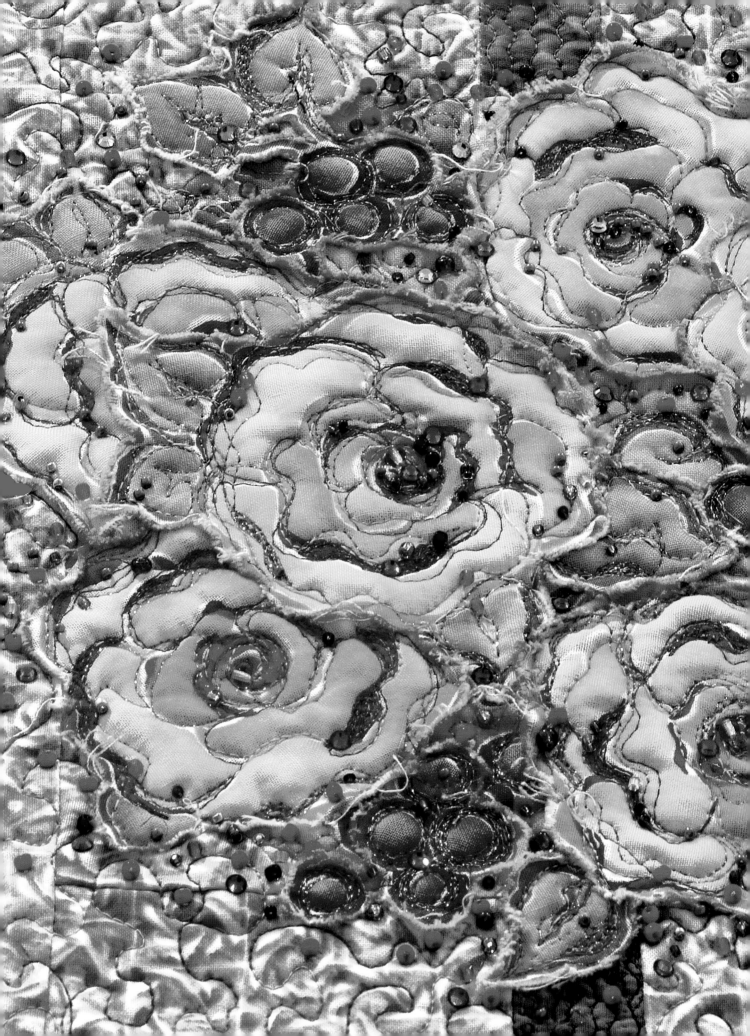

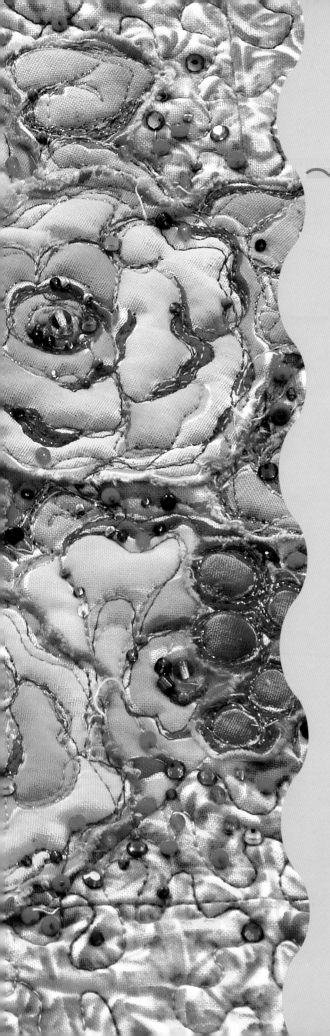

Rose Topiary

Fabric Selection

For the topiary bouquets, I chose a print that looked as if it were hand painted in shades of orange and yellow, with accents of green and purple. Because the background is pieced, I chose a small-scale, overall green print that wasn't directional so that the piecing seams wouldn't be obvious and the green would blend somewhat with the rose print. I added a strip of rose print at the top and the bottom of the wall hanging to echo the roses in the topiary.

Materials

Yardage is based on 42"-wide fabric.

¾ yard of large-scale rose or other floral print for the topiaries, appliqués, and top and bottom border units (yardage may vary, depending on the print, but extra is included for appliqués)

⅓ yard of small-scale print for background

¼ yard or 1 fat quarter of fabric for vase

¼ yard of fabric A for top and bottom border units

⅛ yard of fabric B for bottom border unit

⅛ yard *each* of 1 light and 1 dark fabric for triangle strips in bottom border unit

Small brown scrap for topiary trunk

⅜ yard of fabric for binding

⅝ yard of fabric for backing

⅝ yard of fabric for finished back

20" x 38" piece of lightweight cotton batting

Variegated cotton thread, rayon or polyester thread, and metallic thread to coordinate with fabrics

Assorted seed (round) beads in several sizes and colors

Finished size: 14" x 32"

Give a classic topiary wall hanging new zing with the sparkle of beads and crystals.
Choose a rose print or use any combination of flowers and leaves to create eye-catching
bouquets. This will definitely be a great accent for any spot in your home.

Cutting the Pieces

All measurements include ¼"-wide seam allowances.

From the background fabric, cut:
- 2 strips, 3½" x 42"; crosscut into 2 strips, 3½" x 25½"
- 1 strip, 2½" x 42"; crosscut into:
  4 rectangles, 2½" x 4"
  10 squares, 2½" x 2½"
- 1 strip, 1½" x 42"; crosscut into:
  1 strip, 1½" x 14½"
  2 rectangles, 1½" x 2½"

From the rose print, cut:
- 1 strip, 1½" x 42; crosscut into 2 strips, 1½" x 14½"
- 1 strip, 8½" x 42"; crosscut into 2 squares, 8½" x 8½"

From the brown scrap, cut:
- 2 rectangles, 1½" x 2½"

From the vase fabric, cut:
- 1 strip, 4½" x 42"; crosscut into:
  1 rectangle, 4½" x 8½"
  1 rectangle, 1½" x 4½"

From fabric A, cut:
- 2 strips, 1½" x 14½"

From *each* of the 2 fabrics for the triangle strips, cut:
- 1 strip, 1⅞" x 42"; crosscut into 14 squares, 1⅞" x 1⅞"

From fabric B, cut:
- 1 strip, 1½" x 14½"

From the binding fabric, cut:
- 3 strips, 2½" x 42"

Constructing the Background

1. Draw a diagonal line from corner to corner on the wrong side of the 2½" background squares. With right sides together, position a marked square on each corner of a rose-print square as shown. Stitch on the diagonal lines. Trim ¼" from the stitched line as shown and press the triangles toward the corners. Make two.

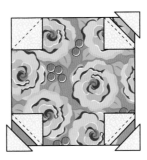

Make 2.

2. Sew the remaining two marked background squares to the bottom corners of the 4½" x 8½" vase rectangle. Trim and press as described in step 1.

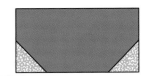

3. Sew a brown rectangle between two 2½" x 4" background rectangles as shown. Make two.

Make 2.

4. Sew the 1½" x 4½" vase rectangle between the two 1½" x 2½" background rectangles as shown.

5. Sew the units from steps 1–4 together as shown to make the topiary unit.

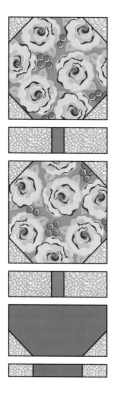
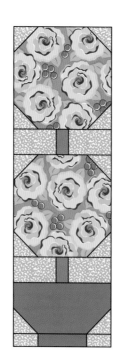

6. Sew the 3½" x 25½" background strips to the sides of the topiary unit.

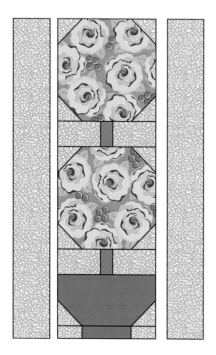

7. Assemble the top border unit. Sew a 1½" x 14½" rose-print strip and a fabric A strip together along the long edges. Press. Sew the unit to the top of the quilt, placing the rose-print strip at the top.

8. To make the triangle strips for the bottom border unit, draw a diagonal line from corner to corner on the wrong side of the 1⅞" light squares. Place each of the marked squares right sides together with a 1⅞" dark square. Stitch ¼" from both sides of the drawn line on each square. Cut on the drawn line. You'll have 28 triangle squares.

Make 28.

9. Sew the triangle squares together as shown. Make two strips. Each strip should measure 14½" long. Sew the triangle strips together along the long edges.

Make 2.

10. Sew the 1½" x 14½" strips of fabrics A and B to opposite sides of the triangle-strip unit. Add the 1½ x 14½" rose-print strip to the bottom of the border unit. Press. Sew the border unit to the bottom of the quilt, placing the rose-print strip at the bottom. Press.

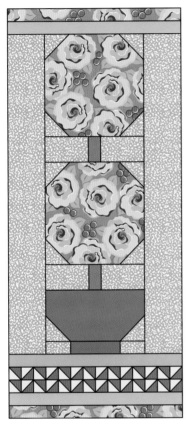

Quilt assembly

Adding the Appliqués

1. Refer to "The Second Layer: Appliqués" on page 17. From the remaining rose print, cut out the appliqué motifs to add to the quilt center. Remember to cut about ⅛" beyond the outer edge of each shape.

2. Position the appliqués on the rose-print topiary blocks, overlapping the edges of the shapes onto the background and adjusting the edges to form a round topiary shape.

3. Add additional appliqués over the top of the rose print if desired. When you're pleased with the arrangement, baste them in place. Press.

4. Refer to "Making the Quilt Sandwich" on page 91 to layer and baste the quilt top, batting, and backing together.

Stitching and Embellishing

1. Refer to "The Third Layer: Decorative Stitching" on page 19. Begin by making the necessary adjustments to the sewing-machine tension, needle, feed dogs, and speed.

2. Use rayon, polyester, or metallic thread to secure the appliqués through the centers and ⅛" from the edges. This will leave the motif edges raw to create texture.

3. Quilt the background and add decorative embroidery detail to the appliqué shapes.

4. Refer to "The Fourth Layer: Beads and Crystals" on page 26. Sew beads to the appliqué motifs and background. Add hot-fix crystals for accents.

Finishing the Quilt

Refer to "Finishing Your Quilt" on page 91 to square up the quilt, add a finished back, bind the edges with the binding strips, and add a hanging sleeve.

Putting on the Glitz: Here's How I Did It

To outline the shapes of the rose petals and flowers, I primarily used metallic threads that coordinated with the flower colors. Because the fabric was nicely shaded, I didn't sew many beads to the petals, but concentrated them in the flower centers and scattered them along the lines of metallic stitching.

I used orange and yellow beads to blend the colors of the flowers with the green background fabric. I did this by sewing a scattering of mostly orange beads—the darkest color in the print—onto the background with a few orange beads on the edges of the flowers themselves. I kept the beads in a circular shape on the background to echo the topiary's round shape.

For the background, I used a variegated green cotton thread to do an overall stippling pattern. I had fun doing a little decorative quilting detail with coordinating threads in the borders.

Gallery

For inspiration, here are a few more Dazzling Quilts, many of which are the creations of other talented quilt artists. They all had fun experimenting with decorative threads, appliqué, and of course, beads or crystal accents for added elegance and pizzazz. Their results are fantastic. Enjoy the tour!

Midnight in the Garden of Glitz and Glitter

Pamela Mostek, Cheney, Washington

Layers and layers of metallic thread give this quilt an aura of sparkle and shine. I placed the crystals in the areas of heavy metallic stitching to further focus on the glitzy threads. I was very pleased when this quilt received an honorable mention in the 2005 Sulky Challenge.

Oriental Poppies

Jean Van Bockel, Coeur d'Alene, Idaho

Jean loves working with lots of vivid colors, and this dramatic quilt is a great example of her masterful use of them. She created her own raw-edged appliqué poppies and embellished them with stitching and a scattering of beads. For an interesting contrast, she used traditional appliqué to add decorative details to the vase.

The Pin Tribe Goes to Market

Carol MacQuarrie, Cheney, Washington

This delightful quilted and embellished bag is perfect for quilt-show shopping, according to Carol. The background of the bag was inspired by "A Garden Wreath" in my book *Scatter Garden Quilts*, but Carol's wonderful eye for color and design gave it her own special touch. The Pin Tribe people were made by her sister, Judy McMillan, and add a fun finishing touch to the bag.

My Mother Was an Artist

Pamela Mostek, Cheney, Washington

I created this elegantly sparkling quilt in memory of my mother, Eula Sims, who taught me to see, appreciate, and create things of beauty. I used primarily hand-dyed silks with a little metallic fabric for accents. I drew the appliqués myself from fabric I had dyed and added beads, crystals, and bits of hand-dyed ribbon. I like to think my mother would have been pleased with the results!

Me and My Sister

Edi Dobbins, Cheney, Washington

The inspiration for this fanciful quilt came when Edi received this fun collection of fabrics for her birthday from her daughter Lydia. She decided to use them to create a quilt as a tribute to her sister Linda, who is also her best friend. All the delightful stitching detail and embellishments make it truly a unique quilt and a delight to examine time and time again!

Garden Path

Debra Lamm, Spokane, Washington

Debra began this quilt with a collection of tropical prints in shades of green and blue. She let the fabric guide her in creating this lovely garden with its winding path and dramatic flower appliqués. She added wonderful machine embroidery and unique beads to give her quilt that special touch of elegance.

Elephant Parade Bag

Pamela Mostek, Cheney, Washington

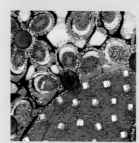

The appliquéd elephants are dressed in their finest beads and sparkling crystals on this fun, festive bag. I used the design of the fabric as the basis for adding lots of metallic thread and crystals to the artist's original design. Hand-dyed ribbons accent the edge of the flap, and beads hang from strips of fabric on the side.

First Frost

Sandra Hawks, Dayton, Washington

Shimmering beads and crystals, highlighted with a sparkling touch of spray glitter, create a frosted look on this lovely pastel wall quilt. Sandy says the embellishments remind her of autumn when flowers are touched with sparkle in the morning after a light frost. Lots of beads, crystals, and ribbon accents complete this very elegant quilt.

September Sky Jacket

**Carol MacQuarrie,
Cheney, Washington**

Carol loves buying fabric, and when she saw this light blue floral, she knew it was destined for something great! She's a talented machine quilter so she did the metallic quilting on her long-arm quilting machine, then cut out the pieces and added the embellishments before she constructed the gorgeous jacket.

Passionate Pink

Pamela Mostek, Cheney, Washington

I could not resist this gorgeous print! I added raw-edged appliqué flowers to cover the border seam, which created a dramatic sense of depth in the quilt. Next came the decorative stitching. This quilt now belongs to Bernina of America and was the inspiration for my collection of Dazzling Quilts.

Latte Dreams

Pamela Mostek, Cheney, Washington

I'm a true coffee lover— but not just ordinary coffee. I have many favorites: lattes, cappuccinos, mochas, and espresso. I love them all! I started with this perfect coffee fabric and then added all the other goodies to make it absolutely delicious. I was pleased to make this quilt for the Association of Pacific Northwest Quilters' traveling exhibit, Spice of Life.

Finishing Your Quilt

The following information will help you give your quilts an attractive, professional finish.

Making the Quilt Sandwich

The quilt "sandwich" consists of the backing, batting, and quilt top. For the projects in this book, the backing should be a lightweight material, such as muslin, so that it will be easier to hand stitch the beads in place. A "finished back" will be added over the backing after the embellishing is done (see the next section).

I recommend that you cut both the batting and backing at least 3" larger than the quilt top on all sides. Because the projects in this book are small, you won't need to piece the backing before layering for most of them. For a larger quilt, you'll need to piece several lengths of fabric together and trim it until it is 3" larger on all sides than the quilt top.

1. Lay the pressed backing, wrong side up, on a clean, flat surface. Follow the manufacturer's instructions to spray the backing with quilt basting spray.

2. Center the batting over the backing, smoothing out any wrinkles and repositioning the batting if necessary.

3. Spray the batting with basting spray and center the pressed quilt top, right side up, over the batting. Smooth out any wrinkles, repositioning the top if necessary.

4. Apply the decorative threads, beads, and crystals as instructed in the project.

Adding the Finished Back

After you have completed the stitching and embellishing of your quilt, the back will undoubtedly look less than perfect! Because of all the detail you're adding to the quilt, which shows on the back side, you will add a second, finished back before you attach the binding. This finishing back can be a gorgeous print that will add further drama to your quilt, and what's even better, you'll look like an absolute master beader because none of your stitches will show on the back of the quilt!

Cut the finished back the same size as you cut the backing. With wrong side up, apply a fusible-web spray, such as OESD's 606 Spray and Fix, to the back, following the manufacturer's instructions. Center the stitched and embellished quilt, right side up, on top of the sprayed back. If you prefer, you can also use an iron-on fusible adhesive such as HeatnBond Lite to fuse on the finished back. Just follow the manufacturer's instructions for application. The binding will hold the backing in place when it is applied.

Squaring Up the Quilt

The heavy quilting and embroidery that you add to your quilt may cause it to shift or pull up in places and make it necessary to square it up before adding the binding. To do that, use a large square ruler, at least 12" x 12", and position it on a corner of the quilt after the finished back has been basted to it. Using a rotary cutter, cut along the edge of the acrylic square, making sure the corner of the quilt is square. This may mean including part of the batting to create a square corner if the edge isn't straight.

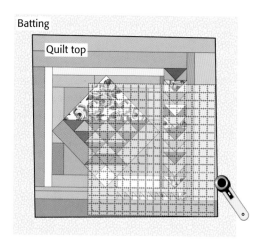

Trim along edge of square ruler.

Repeat to square up all four corners and trim the edges of the backing, batting, and finished back even with the edge of the quilt top.

Adding the Binding

Some of the quilts in the book are finished with a traditional binding that has mitered corners while others have a raw-edge binding with overlapped corners. Choose the method you prefer and refer to the following instructions for each.

Traditional Binding

To make straight-cut, double-layer (French) binding, begin by cutting 2½"-wide strips across the fabric width. You'll need enough strips to go around the perimeter of the quilt, plus about 10" for seams and corners. The number of strips needed has already been calculated for the quilts in this book.

1. With right sides together, sew the strips together on the diagonal as shown to create one long strip. Trim the excess fabric and press the seams open.

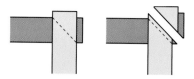

2. Press the strip in half lengthwise, wrong sides together. Cut one end of the strip at a 45° angle and press it under ¼".

3. Beginning on one edge of the quilt and using a ¼"-wide seam allowance, stitch the binding to the quilt, keeping the raw edges even with the quilt-top edge. End the stitching ¼" from the corner of the quilt and backstitch.

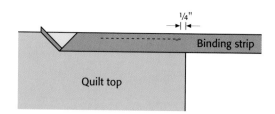

4. Fold the binding up, away from the quilt, then back down onto itself, aligning the raw edges with the quilt edge. Begin stitching at the edge, backstitching to secure, and end ¼" from the lower edge. Repeat the folding and stitching process on the remaining sides.

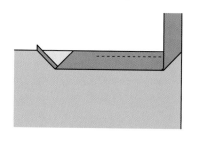

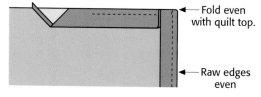

5. When you reach the beginning of the binding, lap the strip over the beginning stitches by about 1" and cut away any excess binding, trimming the end at a 45° angle. Tuck the end of the binding into the fold and complete the seam.

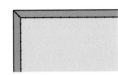

6. Fold the binding to the back. Blindstitch in place, including the miter that forms at each corner.

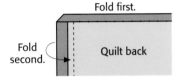

Raw-Edge Binding

The binding is applied separately to each side of the quilt in this method, so you can sew a different fabric binding to each edge of the quilt if you desire. The cutting instructions for each project will indicate the number of 2"-wide strips to cut across the width of the fabric.

1. Measure each side of the quilt. Cut a binding strip for each side that is approximately 1" longer than the measurement.

2. With right sides together, position the side binding strips on the back of the quilt along the side edges, aligning one long edge of the binding with the edge of the quilt. Leave about ½" extending at each end. Stitch the strips to the sides of the quilt, using a ¼" seam allowance.

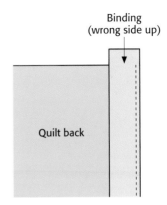

3. Fold the binding strips to the front of the quilt and press. Stitch ¼" to ½" from the binding edge. This will leave the edge raw to create texture. Trim the ends even with the top and bottom edges of the quilt.

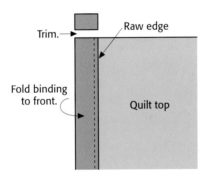

4. Sew the top and bottom binding strips to the quilt in the same manner, overlapping the side binding strips at each end.

Adding a Hanging Sleeve

Because you'll undoubtedly want your Dazzling Quilts to hang so that all can see and enjoy them, it's wise to add a hanging sleeve to the back.

1. Measure the width of the quilt and cut an 8½"-wide strip of fabric the length measured.

2. Press under each short end ¼" and then press under ¼" again. Stitch the hems in place.

3. Press the strip in half lengthwise, wrong sides together.

4. Sew ¼" from the long edges of the sleeve to make a tube. Press the tube so that the seam is centered on the back side of the sleeve and won't show.

Seam hidden at back

5. Center the sleeve at the top of the quilt, just below the edge on the back. Blindstitch along the top and bottom edges, being careful not to stitch through to the front of the quilt.

Quilt back

Quilting Designs

Here are a few patterns to get you started on your free-motion quilting adventure. Remember, small, overall patterns work best for quilting the pieced background.

Resources

Here are a few great online suppliers of embellishments. Be sure to check your local quilt and craft stores as well.

Threads (United Kingdom)

Barnyarns
www.barnyarns.co.uk
Great selection of all kinds of fiber-related treats!

Stef Francis
www.stef-francis.co.uk
Wonderful hand-dyed threads

Texere Yarns
www.www.texere.co.uk
Lots of yummy threads. A catalog that includes samples is available.

Threads (United States)

Oklahoma Embroidery Supply & Design
www.oesd.com
Large range of threads, plus Swarovski crystals, EZ Glitzer jewel applicator wand, and 606 Spray and Fix fusible-web spray

Red Rock Threads
www.redrockthreads.com
Lots of brands, lots of choices, great service

Sewthankful.com
www.sewthankful.com
Fun notions for fiber and thread lovers. Sign up for the weekly newsletter.

Sulky of America
www.sulky.com
Vast array of thread types and colors

Web of Thread
www.webofthread.com
Great variety of thread and great prices. Special offers are available to newsletter subscribers.

Beads and Crystals

Artbeads.com
www.artbeads.com
Beads, crystals, and great customer service

Embroidery Online
www.embroideryonline.com
Swarovski crystals and EZ Glitzer jewel applicator wand

JustBeads.com
www.justbeads.com
An auction site for beads and beaded merchandise

Shipwreck Beads
www.shipwreck.com
More than 38,000 different styles and colors of beads and accessories

About the Author

By her own admission, Pamela Mostek is a true fabriholic, and she is especially passionate about large, dramatic fabrics drenched in color. Her ongoing search to find new ways to show them off inspired *Dazzling Quilts*, her newest book dedicated to this goal.

Her previous books, *Just Can't Cut It!* and *Scatter Garden Quilts*, are also all about using her favorite irresistible fabrics. This time, however, she's added the sparkle and shine of decorative threads, beads, and crystals to the fantastic fabrics to create a new, fresh look for fabric lovers to try.

Putting her degree in art and journalism to good use, Pam spends her time creating quilts for her books and her pattern company, Making Lemonade Designs, as well as designing fabric and teaching. She is the proud mother of two grown daughters and grandmother to four very special grandchildren. She and her husband reside in Cheney, Washington.